The Birth and Death
of a Highland Railu·

CW01082121

British Railways — Scottish Region

TRANSPORT ACT, 1962

WITHDRAWAL OF RAILWAY PASSENGER SERVICES

The British Railways Board hereby give notice, in accordance with Section 56 (7) of the Transport Act, 1962, that on and from 2nd MARCH, 1964, they propose to discontinue the local railway passenger train services

BETWEEN

OBAN, CONNEL FERRY and BALLACHULISH

and to withdraw all passenger services from the following stations:—

*NORTH CONNEL HALT	CREAGAN	KENTALLEN
BENDERLOCH	APPIN	*BALLACHULISH FERRY
BARCALDINE HALT	DUROR	BALLACHULISH

*These stations deal with passenger traffic only and would be closed completely

It appears to the Board that the following alternative services will be available:—

BY RAIL:—
Glasgow trains will continue to serve Oban and Connel Ferry.

BY ROAD:—
An assurance has been given that, subject to the authority of the Traffic Commissioners, road passenger services can be provided at a frequency comparable to the present rail service.

Any user of the rail service at any station from which it is proposed to withdraw ALL passenger services and any body representing such users, desirous of objecting to the proposal, may lodge an objection within six weeks of 5th DECEMBER, 1963, i.e. not later than 17th JANUARY, 1964, addressing any objection to the Secretary of the Transport Users' Consultative Committee for Scotland at 39 George Street, Edinburgh, 2.

THE BIRTH AND DEATH OF
A HIGHLAND RAILWAY

The
Ballachulish
Line

DUNCAN KENNEDY

with additional text by George Simpson

First published in 1971 by John Murray (Publishers) Ltd
This edition, with additional material, published 1996 by House of Lochar

British Library Cataloguing in Publication Data
A catalogue record for this book is available from the British Library

ISBN 1-899863-11-7

Printed in Great Britain by SRP Ltd, Exeter
for House of Lochar, Isle of Colonsay, Argyll PA61 7YR

Contents

Foreword

THE BALLACHULISH RAILWAY was opened to the public on 24th August, 1903, and the last train ran on 26th March, 1966. It was a branch line, which started at Connel Ferry on the Callander and Oban Railway, and ended at Ballachulish. Nearly twenty-eight miles long, it was one of the last lines to be built in Britain towards the end of the railway era. It has been described as the most imposing branch line in the United Kingdom. In my early days, I had, in its construction, learned the elements of my profession, and when I read of the threat of its closure, I felt an urge to place on record something of the way in which that line was built, and what manner of men they were who built it, at a time when rapid changes in methods were impending, but the craftsman had not yet been ousted by the machine.

I had hoped that, as in other cases, the line would be reprieved and live to serve a longer term of usefulness, but a few weeks after I began to write, its doom was sealed, and at short notice it was closed.

This is not a history, which would have driven me to seek out many records, to be meticulous in detail, and in the end perhaps be rather dull. Of written records I have few, and the tale in the main is a tapestry woven from memory, verified in a few important points by reference to old railway records and to the faded columns in the Scottish press of the day that described the opening of the line. At the close of the day I was also able to check up on a few doubtful points of fact through the kindness of the Scottish Records Office in Edinburgh.

The lack of personal records of the building of the line seems to call for some explanation. A couple of years after the First World War had ended, some luggage of mine, consigned to travel home from abroad by sea, went down in the Mediterranean along with the ship that carried it. Among other things, it contained an assortment of books, papers and useful records of previous experience, such as one accumulates and carries around from one temporary place of abode to another, when engaged in the construction of public works in far places. At a later date, when the Second World War had begun, my office in East Africa was burned to the ground with all its contents, which included not only another twenty years' accumulation of records but also some few items that had escaped the earlier catastrophe.

If therefore in any factual detail my memory has played me false, I ask the reader's forbearance, and I can only hope that any slips I have made are not of sufficient importance to mar the overall picture. I did try to be more objective in my approach, but found this very difficult. Even as the young elephant in India and the boy destined to be its mahout are brought up together and their mutual interests are intertwined, so the Ballachulish Railway and the budding civil engineer spent five of their formative years in each other's company, and I found that when I tried to deal with one of them apart, the other had an incurable habit of butting in.

I have here and there included patches of local colour that may help to picture the way of life that existed before the coming of the railway. I have also included some bits of earlier local history, for it is often such things that attract the visitor from outside and so create the need to provide for his transport, by whatever means he travels, road or rail.

As for the running of the line itself, beyond the first year of its operation I have had nothing to say, for during the heyday of its fortunes and through the period of slow decline to its final end I was 'over the hills and far away' and out of touch.

The last chapter deals with the closing of the line.

The scarcity of photographs of the railway works during and after construction is much regretted. The lack of those I took myself is partly explained by the destruction through flood and fire referred to above. Many good pictures must have been taken by other people, but exhaustive enquiries have failed to find them.

DK, 1971

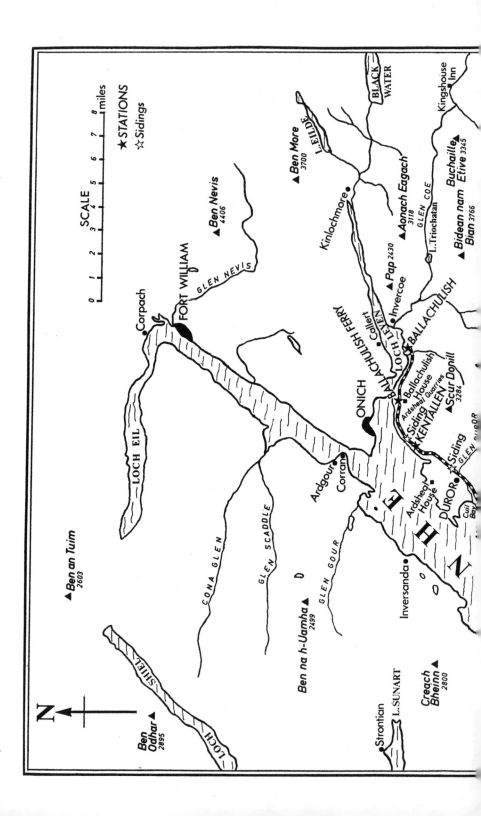

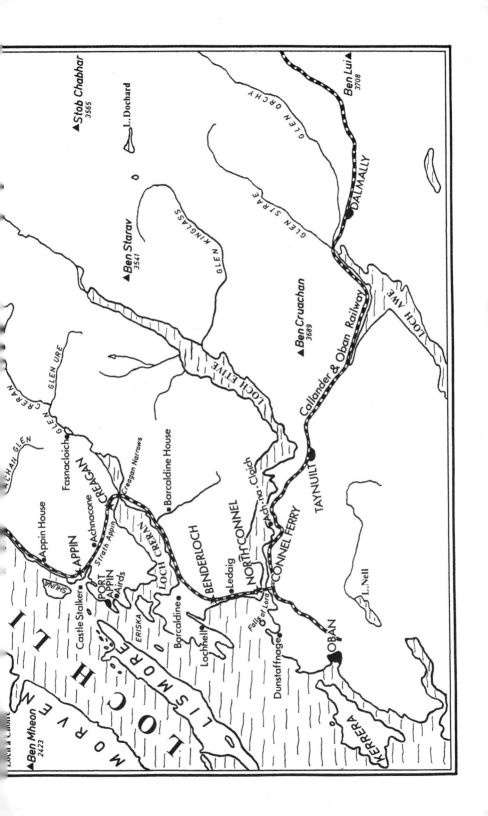

PASS OF GLENCOE, GLEN ETIVE AND LOCH ETIVE DAY TOUR

TRAIN TO BALLACHULISH (GLENCOE): MOTOR VIA GLENCOE TO LOCHETIVEHEAD: YACHT "DARTHULA II" ON LOCH ETIVE TO ACHNACLOICH AND TRAIN HOME

or the route may be reversed

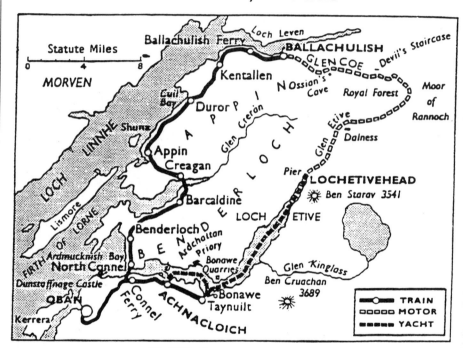

FARES FOR THE ROUND

From	1st Class Rail	2nd Class Rail	From	1st Class Rail	2nd Class Rail
Achnacloich	16/9	15/–	§Dalmally	22/9	18/9
§Appin	16/9	15/–	§Duror	16/9	15/–
Ballachulish (Glencoe)	16/9	15/–	‡Fort William	*20/–	*18/3
§Ballachulish Ferry	16/9	15/–	§Kentallen	16/9	15/–
§Benderloch	16/9	15/–	§Loch Awe	21/6	18/–
Connel Ferry	16/9	15/–	Oban	19/3	16/6
§Creagan	16/9	15/–	Taynuilt	18/3	16/–

* Juvenile fares—10/3, 1st Class Rail; 9/3, 2nd Class Rail.

§ Passengers from these Stations travel by train to connect with the services shown.

‡ Passengers from Fort William travel by Messrs. MacBrayne's motor to connect with the tour at Ballachulish Ferry.

The tickets are valid on the date for which issued

FOR TRAIN, MOTOR AND YACHT TIMES SEE OPPOSITE PAGE

(For route map and fares see opposite page)

PASS OF GLENCOE, GLEN ETIVE AND LOCH ETIVE DAY TOUR

TRAIN, MOTOR AND YACHT TIMES

Going via Ballachulish

T R A I N

		a.m.	
Oban	leave	9 30	
Connel Ferry	„	9 54	
Ballachulish (Ferry)	„	11 5	
Ballachulish (Glencoe)	arrive	11 12	

M O T O R

		a.m.	
Ballachulish (Glencoe)	leave	11 15	
Lochetivehead	arrive	1 15p	

Y A C H T   " D A R T H U L A   II "

		p.m.	
Lochetivehead	leave	1 45	
Taynuilt Pier	arrive	3 0	
Achnacloich	„	3 45	

T R A I N

		p.m.	
Achnacloich	leave	4 9	
Connel Ferry	arrive	4 17	

		p.m.	p.m.
Connel Ferry	leave	4 20	5 20
Oban	arrive	4 37	—
Ballachulish Ferry	„	—	6 31
Ballachulish (Glencoe)	„	—	6 37

Going via Achnacloich

T R A I N

		a.m.	
Oban	leave	9 18	
Connel Ferry	„	9 36	
Achnacloich	arrive	9 44	

Y A C H T   " D A R T H U L A   II "

		a.m.	
Achnacloich	leave	10 15	
Taynuilt Pier	„	10 45	
Lochetivehead	arrive	12 30p	

M O T O R

		p.m.	
Lochetivehead	leave	1 20	
Ballachulish (Glencoe)	arrive	3 30	

T R A I N

		C	D
		p.m.	p.m.
Ballachulish (Glencoe)	leave	3 38	3 48
Connel Ferry	arrive	4 54	5 4
Oban	„	5 32	5 35

C Ceases after 15th June.   D Commences 17th June.

Note:—Fort William Passengers travel outward by Messrs MacBraynes Motor leaving 9.35 a.m. and arriving North Ballachulish 10.15 a.m. Return motor leaves North Ballachulish at 6.50 p.m. and arrives Fort William 7.30 p.m. (Passengers make their own way by ferry between North Ballachulish and Ballachulish Ferry and to and from Ballachulish Ferry Station).

Illustrations

Plate 1 The author and his twin brothers; The Dirty Cutting; The diver at Creagan

Plate 2 The navvy; The ganger (*from drawings by D.T. Rose*)

Plate 3 Work on a side cutting; Hand drilling (*from drawings by D.T. Rose*)

Plate 4 Creagan Bridge (*Valentine, Dundee*); Connel Ferry Bridge and the Falls of Lora (*Crown Copyright*)

Plate 5 Connel Ferry Bridge under construction (*photo in the possession of John Farrow*)

Plate 6 Benderloch Station in operation (*Valentine, Dundee*); MacBrayne's paddle steamer at Corpach (*Graham E. Langmuir*)

Plate 7 Next stop Appin: 30 October 1961; Crossing Creagan Bridge: 9 February 1962 (*George N. Simpson*)

Plate 8 Taking water at Creagan Station: a Sunday in November 1961; Summer excursion train departing Creagan Station, 30 June 1962 (*George N. Simpson*)

Notes on Plates 7 and 8

7 *(top)* Caledonian Class 2P, 0–4–4 Tank loco No. 55204 hauls the 12.30pm Connel Ferry to Ballachulish passenger train away from Creagan Station, up the gradient towards Invernahyle at 12.55pm . These little tank locos were affectionately known by the footplate crew as 'Pugs', and No. 55204 was the last of its type to leave Oban, after dieselisation in Summer 1962.

7 *(bottom)* British Railways Standard Class 2MT, 2–6–0 loco No. 78052 crossing Creagan Bridge with the 12.30pm Connel Ferry to Ballachulish passenger train. The footway bolted onto the eastern side of Creagan Bridge can be seen to the left of the picture. An unusual feature is that the loco is chimney/smokebox first, whereas normally locos running northbound to Ballachulish, in charge of passenger trains, would run bunker/tender first, after having reversed around their trains at Connel Ferry.

8 *(top)* Ivatt LMS *Mogul* (1946) Class 2MT, 2–6–0, locomotive No 46460 quenching its thirst at Creagan Station. This loco is taking a break from duty while in charge of a ballast train upgrading track at Invernahyle, to replenish the water tank, located in its tender. Loco 46460, a newcomer to the Ballachulish Branch, was one of a batch of three similar types introduced in Summer 1961 only one year before dieselisation, to strengthen the aged fleet of Caledonian Class 2P 0–4–4 tank locos which, in the main, handled all passenger traffic.

8 *(bottom)* On a misty morning, BRC&W, Sulzer Type 2 diesel locomotive No. D5357 departs from Creagan Station at 10.30am in charge of the 9.42am Oban–Ballachulish (Glencoe) Summer excursion train, forming part of the Pass of Glencoe, Glen Etive and Loch Etive circular tour which involved train, motorbus and yacht. The Camping Coach, in the rear siding of Creagan Station, can be seen in the background.

I

The Beginning

IT WAS a fine autumn morning when I left the house. Some of the leaves were turning, and the stubble fields were mostly bare. There was a fresh nip in the air: a good morning to be starting anything. But my mind was too preoccupied with other things to enjoy what the day was offering.

Two miles up the road I saw the first signs of the activity I was looking for. Just beyond the general store at Kentallen a gang of men had started to open out a cutting on the hillside. One of them, in response to an enquiry, pointed out the ganger. The ganger referred me to somebody he called the 'traveller', but seeing that I didn't understand, he explained it was the 'walking ganger', who had been here a few minutes before and was just round the corner. The walking ganger was more informative. I should probably find the engineer, Mr. Rose, about two miles further on where he lodged, and he directed me to the place.

Mr. Rose was at home, and obviously using his bedroom as an office: a tall, friendly sort of man of about twenty-eight, with a manner that was quietly competent, but somewhat reserved. I told him I wanted to be a civil engineer. I gave him my history and asked if he could help me. He thought he could. I could come along any time and make a start, but he would have to see Mr. Wilson for confirmation. They would probably pay me about fifteen shillings a week. I did not know it, but that was the beginning of a lifelong friendship.

When I left Mr. Rose and turned for home again, there was a lilt in the step and a lightness of heart that had not been there before. As I swung along the road, I was able now to review with quiet satisfaction the events and frustrations that had led me up to this.

It was two years since I had finished with the local school. Soon after I left, there had been a report that my old schoolmaster, Mr. Macgregor, grey-bearded and one-armed, was going to start evening classes when the winter set in. I made haste to call upon him, but the master quickly disillusioned me.

'This is not for you,' he said, 'I've taught you all I know.'

A few weeks later I lost my father. Before he died he handed over to me his system of accounts, simple but effective. It has been the basis all my life of such accounting as my professional duties demanded, when skilled accountancy was lacking.

Just when the urge to be a civil engineer first possessed me it would be hard to say, for I had never met one. Perhaps it had its origin in my very early days, when I had heard my mother speak of a relative of hers called Paterson, who had been an engineer in the north before my time.

There were various methods of getting a training. One was to pay a substantial sum, probably in guineas, to a consulting engineer who would take you into his office for a period of years, and perhaps pay you nothing till your pupillage was completed. That was ruled out for me as I had not access to the necessary guineas for fee and maintenance. Another method was to take a university degree to start with and get practical training afterwards. This, at the time, was not very popular, as many employers thought a man was wasting his best years at the university when he should be in an office or out on works getting practical experience.

This attitude was illustrated to me later on, soon after I had started my training, by a remark of one of the section engineers. 'You are lucky,' he said. 'My brother took his degree and then had to wait two years before he got a job.' It was not only in Britain that a university degree was suspect: a few years later in Montreal, an engineer of about my own vintage told me that he had taken his degree in Glasgow before he went to Canada. 'But I didn't tell anyone here,' he said. 'My name would have been mud!' In this connection, it is interesting to note that of the thirty-six engineers who, up to the end of the last century, had held, in succession, the position of President of the Institution of

Civil Engineers—the highest position in his profession to which a civil engineer in this country can aspire—only one appears to have taken a university degree.

Anyhow, a university course cost quite a bit of money, and any competitive bursaries for which I had entered before leaving school had all been appropriated by cleverer youngsters than I. There were other concerns such as the railway companies who took on pupils in their engineering offices for a period of four or five years without fees, and paid them a small nominal wage during their training. Their theoretical work these pupils studied after working hours, either at evening classes or at home. There was a long waiting list for such vacancies.

Since those days the taking of a university degree has become much more general. The financial path of the student has been made more smooth by Government grants, and the differing views as to the relative merits of theory and practice in early training have been largely discounted by one form or another of what is called the 'sandwich' course that some universities have adopted. The student spends part of the period of his university course at his academic studies and part on practical training. Perhaps the most effective form of sandwich is to divide each year of the course in this way. The student thus has an opportunity of relating theory to practice as he goes along, and he can also, while at a very receptive stage, get a closer insight into the practical details of the work than he would ever be likely to get after graduation.

Nevertheless, by whatever means the civil engineer gained his training in those early days of which I write, at the turn of the century, his status was high in public esteem, a position that some consider has not been maintained in more recent times.

It was sometime during that first year after I had left school that a survey party worked through the district, setting out the line of a new branch railway that was to link Connel Ferry with Ballachulish. It would run slap through our fields for nearly half a mile, so here was the promise of engineering brought right to the door. My old school friend, Sandy, a son of Canon Mac-Kenzie, got a job with the surveyors as chainman, and I made haste to join him. We spent a glorious three weeks, working under a man called Schreiber. He was a capable surveyor and a martinet, and he kept us on our toes. He was said to have come from Canada, although in speech and appearance he seemed more the type one came to recognise later as the public-school Englishman. Perhaps his Canadian experience accounted for his fondness for using an axe for all sorts of purposes—lopping a tree branch, knocking in a peg or sharpening a lead pencil, and the edge had to be kept razor sharp. Actually, interference with any growing tree was severely frowned on except when unavoidable. The reason was succinctly put by a local landowner, when at a later date his claim for compensation was being considered: 'You can knock a tree down in half an hour. It takes forty years to grow it.'

Another member of 'other ranks' was the lad Isaiah, usually hailed by our chief as 'Bo-oy'. He carried the spare gear when it was not in use—poles, pegs, axe and other impedimenta, usually clasped tightly to his body with both arms, so that he often looked like a walking assembly of ancient weapons, such as one sees on the walls of museums or baronial halls. The boy, undaunted by occasional rebuke, had an irrepressible store of humour deep down in his system, which tended, when the chief was out of earshot, to come bubbling up at unexpected moments, and kept life from becoming too serious. Over the rise from the man at the theodolite would come a hail for the man with the ranging rod: 'Tell him I can only see to the bottom of his waistcoat.' Relayed by Isaiah the message would arrive: 'He can see down to the bottom of your whiskers!' His brother, John, a steady lad of about twenty, was with us for a few days. In virtue of his manhood, John was supposed to use the five-pound axe. 'That's a boy's axe you're using,' Schreiber admonished him on one occasion, referring to the three-pounder—a lovely tool—that he had picked up to knock in a peg.

Much of this part of the line was through rough and rocky ground, resulting in numerous curves, with short intervening straights. The setting out of the centre line had already been completed for over twenty miles from the Connel end, and this work we were now continuing. We measured with a hundred-foot chain, and at each hundred feet, measured horizontally, a small peg was driven, with a larger peg behind it carrying a painted index number. On one or two wet days we stayed indoors, painting the numbers on the pegs. The beginning and end of curves were marked with three pegs, the outer ones slanting, so that if any two were lost the remaining one could easily be identified. For other measurements, a linen tape was used conveniently marked in feet and tenths of a foot, which was halfway to the metric system, and proved a great timesaver.

Where the public road ran parallel and reasonably near to the line, it was one of our functions to measure all drains and culverts passing under the road, keeping a sharp lookout for any signs of overflowing. From this information the provision that had to be made for the passing of streams under the railway could be assessed.

It was a profitable period, though short, and it was surprising how quickly one mastered the minor skills—to hold a levelling staff or ranging rod plumb when standing on the side of a hill, to pace a hundred feet on the level correctly to within a few inches, and to chain a mile over ground of varying roughness, also to within inches. I well remember an occasion on which we had to re-chain a mile, and found a discrepancy of about two feet between the two measurements. Mr. Schreiber told us in no uncertain terms what he thought of us, but neither Sandy nor I was unduly depressed, for on that occasion we had been energetically helped by a young assistant engineer from the head office, and we had a feeling that the scorching we got was not entirely for our benefit.

This brief contact with practical engineering did but whet the appetite for more. Glasgow, to the Western Highlands, was the metropolis, the centre of much activity, engineering and otherwise. But to us out there among the hills, sixteen miles by road to the nearest railway station, with two ferries to cross on the way, Glasgow was not in those days so easy of access. By road there was no public transport. The best way was to go by one of MacBrayne's paddle steamers from Ballachulish pier. If you wished to reach Glasgow before the day was far spent, you got up about three in the morning, had breakfast and were driven in the trap five miles to catch the six o'clock steamer that reached Oban about eight. There you could change to a train that got you to Glasgow in the early afternoon; or to a succession of steamers—Oban to Crinan, Crinan through the canal in the little *Linnet* to Ardrishaig, and Ardrishaig to the Clyde by that queen of the fleet the *Columba*, which got you to Glasgow in the late evening. Our visits to Glasgow were few.

I had an uncle in the city, a brother of my father's, and a lawyer by profession, who knew some of the railway people, and kindly made enquiries on my behalf. The engineer of the northern division of the Caledonian Railway, a man called Barr, with an office in Perth, was a friend of his, and very willing to be helpful. But he wrote that engineering at the time was passing through a difficult phase, because of the lack of new work. He himself had just taken on a new pupil who had been on the waiting list for nearly a year, and during that period there had been five or six other applicants. Mr. Barr promised to take up my case with his fellow divisional engineers and with some other offices in Glasgow, but he made it clear that as things stood, it might be a long wait. He was right.

2

Marking Time

IN THE MEANTIME I continued being busy on the three square
miles or so of mountain, heather and strath that my forebears had
farmed for sixty years. 'Busy' is not entirely a figurative word.
Restrictive practices had not yet been introduced, nor had 'summer
time' been thought of. The working day on the land was spread
over the whole twenty-four hours, as occasion demanded, for
six days in the week, and as few hours as possible on the seventh.

For example, in the long summer days, when a gathering of
the sheep took place, one had to be at the head of the glen around
three in the morning, so as to start the slow homeward drive as
soon as the dawning light permitted. This meant leaving home
about one o'clock, and some did not bother to go to bed at all.
The flock, filling the air with their lamentations, would reach the
hillside above the fank about six. After some sorting out of
stragglers from other farms there was breakfast, and then the real
work of the day began, shearing, marking or whatever was the
purpose of the gathering.

The day ended when the work was finished, perhaps about six,
and then the neighbours who had tramped over the hill to give
a hand for the occasion, called their dogs, collected the stragglers
from their own flocks and tramped home again. We, the younger
members, who had not taken part in the drive, might find our
way to the river, and in the coolness of a deep pool, wash away
the grime and sweat of the day. These gatherings were not
frequent, but I have heard a neighbour complain that he had risen
every morning at three for a period of six weeks to have a look
at the weather, and then had to abandon his programme each
morning because of the rain, or the threat of it, and return to
bed. Rain and shearing do not go together.

It was usual for the staff to take the same keen interest in the work of the farm as did the family, and I recall an occasion when the ploughman, returning late at night from a ceilidh, and seeing great banks of thunder cloud massing on the horizon, roused all hands, family and servants, to go out with lanterns and secure a field of stooked oats before the storm broke.

When the harvest was secured (a matter that like most operations depended on the weather), the winter ploughing was started. The lambs of that year, which were now classed as hoggs, were brought in from the hill to winter on the low ground, and roamed over the unfenced fields and rough grazing that adjoined them. Daily it was now necessary to walk round the strath and look for casualties, or release any that had been caught by the wool in the occasional brier. The rams were also brought in, herded and hand-fed till a prearranged date when they were released to the hill again to mate with the ewes. When on the low ground they sometimes passed their time in trials of strength. Two rams would back steadily away from each other till they were perhaps twenty or thirty yards apart, then stop and charge like tilting knights till they met head on with a resounding clash of their great curling horns. Then back to have another go till one had enough and broke off the engagement.

Throughout the winter the hill had to be visited daily to look for trouble among the sheep and, in the earlier weeks, to ensure that the rams were all on duty and had not strayed across the boundary to pay court to a neighbour's ewes.

All the cattle except the milking cows and a few calves had summered on the hill—young stock and Highland cows, long-haired and long-horned, with calves at foot. These were all brought under cover at night during the winter, and had to be fed like the others with oat straw, hay and turnips. Thrashing of the straw and the morning feeding were daily carried out before breakfast. Except in very severe weather, all cattle were turned out to graze during the day. The chilly winter days closed in to seven or eight hours of daylight, and the operations of thrashing, of feeding and milking cattle and of feeding and grooming horses extended at both ends of the day into the lamplit hours.

Spring brought the earth's awakening, seedtime and the rich smell of farmyard manure spread over the land. The first lambs came, and for some weeks, the shepherd's life was a full one. Crook in hand and telescope slung over his shoulder, he must be on the hill at dawn, and twice a day he quartered the rough miles to ensure that he overlooked no lambing ewe that needed his help. It was frustrating to find in the afternoon the bodies of a ewe and her half-born lamb lying in a slight depression of the ground, the eyes of both picked out by the hoodie-crows, where in the morning he had passed unwitting on the other side of the knoll. Motherless lambs had to be carried home, and a ewe that had lost her own lambs was penned for a time with an orphan, dressed up in the skin of her dead child like a little waistcoat, to give her the scent she knew, until it was quite sure that she accepted the substitute as her own.

But life was not by any means all work. Occasional day visits by steamer to the nearer towns, Oban or Fort William, for markets or other business, or less frequently just for pleasure, made a break in the routine of the day's work. When the weather was too broken for work outside, one might, in the season, take a rod and spend a few hours on the swollen river, returning with a fresh-run sea trout or a few brown trout for the next morning's breakfast. There was some grouse, ptarmigan and mixed shooting on the hill. We usually let the shooting to a tenant, but when he had gone there was always something left if one cared to walk out with a gun. Hares came down in the winter, and there were rabbits in the strath. The horrors of myxomatosis had not yet been discovered, but with two or three keen young hunters to deal with them when time permitted, and curried rabbit being a popular dish with us, there never seemed to be any difficulty in keeping the rabbits under control.

We rented the small island of Balnagowan, lying out in Cuil Bay about three-quarters of a mile from the shore. In the spring, we ferried across to the island a dozen or so of year-old stirks that had not wintered too well, some our own and some bought locally, and left them there for a year. A score of old ewes were also put across to fatten. We had two rowing boats, one a heavy craft for ferrying the stock and the other a light skiff for periodic visits and general purposes. On their way out most of the stirks would be taken on board, but on their return a year later, as great hairy two-year-olds, they had to work their passage and swim behind the boat, three or four at a time, attached to halter ropes that two men held in the stern. If any loafer tried to evade his obligations and hang on the rope, the remedy was to slack off and give his head a shove under water. It was surprising with what alacrity he came up snorting and energetic, and got his legs into action again.

There was no water on the island, but everything seemed to thrive, and casualties among the stock were rare. By the time they were due to return to the mainland, however, they were getting pretty wild, and there was often a bit of trouble in getting them penned in the stout little enclosure where they had to be roped. On one very hot day a sheep broke away after a lot of rounding up and made for the sea. One of my brothers stripped in haste and swam out to intercept her, while the other two of us got the boat out and rowed it round the head. By the time we reached her, the ewe was inert. We hauled her on board, and the swimmer, who had medical aspirations, did his best to restore her by artificial respiration. He expelled a lot of seawater from her insides, but there was no other result.

The island was a favourite breeding ground for innumerable seabirds—gulls, terns, guillemots, eider duck and lots of others. Whether for duty or pleasure, it was always a joy to visit it, and the nostalgic music of the calling birds lingers long in the memory. In the nesting season, the music changed to an excited clamour for the safety of eggs or chicks, and the intruder was liable to be startled by the sudden rush of a large bird, swooping close to his head.

Our social contacts with the outside world were chiefly confined to the summertime, when friends came to visit us and many city dwellers spent their holidays in the district. Occasionally there were more unusual visitors. There was a geologist named Grant Wilson, a large and friendly person, who in the course of his duties lodged with us for some months. He was said to have only one lung, but if so, this did not deter him from setting out in the morning, appropriately clad in knickerbockers, haversack on shoulder with his sandwiches and little hammer, and spending a long day on the hill. He did not usually talk much about his work, but I remember one summer evening when we strolled out with him on the hillside, and he pointed out to us the striations on the rock surface caused by the slow-moving ice that covered the land in the glacial periods.

He was joined at one time for a few weeks by a much younger man, a strapping fellow named Bailey, who must have been somewhat ahead of his time: he was the first grown man I had ever seen wearing shorts.

On another occasion I was alone about the place one day when the minister of the Church of Scotland, the Reverend James McDougall, arrived in a state of suppressed excitement, accompanied by a dignified and courteous gentleman, whom he introuced to me with a mixture of pride and awe as Mr. Andrew Lang. I had, no doubt, come across the name before, but it did not convey much to me. However, judging by the minister's manner, I concluded he must be a man of some importance in whatever was his walk in life.

Mr. Lang, it appeared, was interested in the historic background to an incident that had occurred in the district and came to be known as the Appin Murder. The incident had been described by R. L. Stevenson in his fascinating romance *Kidnapped*, published a dozen years earlier. Lang was no doubt intrigued by the story, and he must also have been at the time amassing material for his *History of Scotland*, which was issued in four volumes soon after the turn of the century, but in the event did not cover much ground beyond the battle of Culloden Moor.

The victim of the murder was one Captain Colin Campbell of Glenure, and the year 1752, some six years after Culloden, that sealed for ever the fate of the Jacobite cause. On that grim field many of the Appin Stewarts who had fought for Prince Charlie lost their lives. Stewart of Ardsheal, a reigning chieftain among them, was exiled. His lands were forfeited, and his tenants obliged to pay their rents to the hated Hanoverian government.

Campbell of Glenure undertook to collect the rents. He appears to have been an honest man, but nevertheless, was a member of a clan which had supported the Hanover cause, and which was much hated by the Stewarts.

James Stewart, commonly known as James of the Glen ('Seamus a Ghlinne' in the Gaelic), was a half-brother of the exiled Ardsheal, and with him had followed the Prince. He farmed the lands of Acharn, and was a man of influence among his fellow-clansmen in the district. Between him and the factor, who was but doing his duty, there was at first no cause for enmity, and Glenure was glad to use the knowledge and ability of James in his dealings with the tenants.

James, understandably, whenever he could, leased the farms to Jacobites, and in due course the Commissioners for Forfeited Estates blamed Glenure for this. In the spring of 1752 a number of the tenants got notice to quit. Bad feelings were aroused between Glenure and James of the Glen, and James went through to Edinburgh to oppose the removals. His appeal failed, and on 14th May, the day before the Whitsun term, Campbell of Glenure, accompanied by a sheriff officer, an Edinburgh lawyer and a manservant, crossed the ferry at Ballachulish, on their way to carry out the evictions. They were all unarmed. As they went along the old road near Lettermore, Glenure and the lawyer on horseback, the others on foot, a shot was fired from the hillside above, and Glenure fell, mortally wounded.

There was a great hue and cry. A Campbell had been murdered in Stewart country, and someone must be found to pay the price. James of the Glen and several others were arrested, and the events that followed have been described as a sordid travesty of justice. The Argyll Circuit Court did not open till September, some four months after the murder, and all means were employed by the prosecution to prevent an earlier trial, as this would have had to take place in Edinburgh before an unprejudiced jury.

At length the trial of James Stewart was begun on 21st September in Inverary, before a jury of Campbells, with the Duke of Argyll, the greatest Campbell of them all, sharing the bench with two other judges of lesser weight. James, on the most questionable evidence, was found guilty of the murder, and on 8th November he was hanged on a low hill to the south of Ballachulish Ferry. The body was left hanging in chains, with a guard constantly on duty to prevent its removal for burial, until many weeks afterwards the skeleton mysteriously disappeared. A monument now marks the spot.

Quoting from David McKay in his book *The Appin Murder* ' "James Stewart," says Mr. Andrew Lang, "was, to speak plain words, judicially murdered." '

There were many sordid and brutal events in the history of the warring Highland clans, and it is likely that the Appin murder would long ago have been forgotten, except in the district immediately concerned, were it not that R. L. Stevenson touched the story with the magic of his pen and ensured that for a long time to come it would be remembered by English-speaking people, and by many of other tongues who had read translations of his books.

I showed Andrew Lang and the minister over James's old house. It was a one-storied building about sixty feet long and twenty wide, with walls of solidly-built stone and mortar, and divided into two by a partition wall of similar construction. One gable wall and the partition had fireplaces with chimneys. When first I knew it the roof had been thatched, and supported on the original old rough-hewn oak trusses, but some time in the nineties an inquisitive Highland bull had found his way in by an open door and brought the roof down. This had been replaced by a corrugated iron roof with deal trusses, and minor repairs had been made to the side walls. Now one end was used for the housing of peats and various oddments, while the other, divided into two by a wooden partition, served as an out-kitchen and an overflow dormitory, when the summer influx of visitors crowded us out of the house.

The sea was about a mile away, and occasionally when time permitted we rowed out in the bay, anchored and fished with handlines. At other times, in the long summer evenings, we would row slowly along with bamboo or home-made rods and trailing flies, the flies either on the surface or a couple of feet below, with the rod slowly churned up and down in the water. No great stuff for an angler, but a refreshing change after a day on the land, and we generally carried home a good string of saith ('cuddies' they were locally called), lythe and perhaps a few mackerel.

Every season had its special charm as well as its special work. But apart from the pleasure of having our summer visitors, I think winter was my favourite season. The clouds and mist came down on the hills when it rained, but low-lying fog was practically unknown. I loved the snow; we made our own toboggans. And when a spell of frosty weather came we enjoyed a climate that the town dweller does not know, huddling with his fellows through the winter in the fogs and foul air of his antheap, and escaping to countryside or seaside for his brief summer holiday. The sun shone, the sky was blue, the crystal air was crisp and still. The streams froze over and every little waterfall was changed overnight into a fairyland of hanging icicles. If there had been soft snow before the frost, the stillness of the glen might be broken by the soft tinkle of bells that came from the row of little iceballs that fringed each fleece, as the sheep moved, foraging among the half-covered heather. It was good to be alive.

It was, however, a hard period for those who had to make their living from the land. They had to compete with new territories being opened up in the West, where too often the virgin soil was being exploited for immediate results, and drained of its accumulated store of richness, with no regard to the future. As a result, prices of farm produce in the homeland fell below the cost of production, and many left for the cities or to go abroad.

Well, for me all that was now a thing of the past. The front door of my chosen profession had been closed to me; I had patiently besieged the side entrance without success for the best part of two years—two years too many. Now I had quietly pushed open the back door and got my foot inside.

3

Staff and Organisation

MR. WILSON duly confirmed my appointment, with the proviso that fifteen shillings a week was far too much for a chap who was being taught his profession, and he promptly knocked it down to ten.

I soon learned the set-up of the contractor's organisation. Over the whole contract was the Agent, who in this case was Mr. Allan Best, a son of John Best, the contractor, and was usually referred to as 'The Boss'. Mr. Wilson was the contractor's chief engineer, a man in his early thirties, and under him were three section engineers, each with a stretch of nine or ten miles of line to look after, in the sense of seeing that the work was carried out true to line and level, was in accordance with the specification and was properly measured and billed. David Rose, my immediate chief, had the Ballachulish section. Actual supervision of the labour was the job of the walking ganger, so called because his work took him all over the section and he was always on the move. There was a cashier, and each section had a timekeeper.

I was fortunate in those early chiefs of mine, first Schreiber, the surveyor, and then Wilson and Rose, each an able man in his own way and a good man to work for. Rose, I found, was also a keen artist, and his work had either already been, or was later, exhibited at the Royal Academy.

There was, I also soon discovered, a parallel engineering staff on the site. The Callander and Oban Railway Company employed consulting engineers, whose function it was to look after their interests in the building of the new branch line. In the early stages the consulting engineers had surveyed the land, advised on the route to be selected, designed the works, estimated the cost and set out the centre line. They had prepared drawings, specifications and bills of quantities for the letting of a contract, and advised on the tenders received and the selection of one for acceptance. They now supervised the construction of the work to ensure that the contractor fulfilled his contract, and to measure and certify for payment the quantity of work done.

Sir John Wolfe Barry was consulting engineer. He was a man with a distinguished background. His father, Sir Charles Barry, R.A., was the well-known architect, and designed the Houses of Parliament. Sir John himself came early to prominence, and among his notable works was the building of the Tower Bridge across the Thames. In this work he was at first associated with Sir Horace Jones as architect, but Sir Horace died soon after the work began, and after that Wolfe Barry carried almost the entire responsibility. He had a world-wide reputation, and it was said of him that his work was known from China to Peru. In the years 1896–8 he was President of the Institution of Civil Engineers. He was consulting engineer for the Caledonian Railway in connection with various works in the Glasgow area. The fact that his early education had been received at Glenalmond School in Perthshire would no doubt be an added factor to link his sympathies with the Scottish scene.

In close association with Sir John Wolfe Barry on the Ballachulish branch was the Glasgow firm of Formans and McCall, of which Mr. Charles Forman was the leading partner. The association between the two firms had been active in much of the work for which Forman had been responsible for several years before the Ballachulish work was started. He was a man of strong personality, determined, competent and resourceful. When he died, an obituary notice stated:

'The firm has been continually associated with the development of the railway system in the west of Scotland, and through Mr. Forman's energy and ability this undoubtedly received a decided impulse: in various instances long-talked-of enterprises were formulated successfully, conducted through Parliament, and eventually carried out under his guidance.'

When first I heard of him, he was said to have aspired in his work to 'make two blades of grass grow where one had grown before'. I thought then that the phrase was his own, but long afterwards I came across it again in a book that was written more than a hundred years before his time. In *Gulliver's Travels* the hero of the story tells that the king of Brobdingnag 'gave it for his opinion, that whoever could make two ears of corn or two blades of grass to grow upon a spot of ground where only one grew before, would deserve better of mankind, and do more essential service to his country, than the whole race of politicians put together'. But whoever originated the saying, the fact that Charles Forman should have been heard to quote it purposefully gives an indication of the kind of man he was. I was never privileged to meet him. He died in 1901, a young man of forty-eight.

The work was carried on by his partners, Mr. J. E. Harrison and Mr. John Ferguson. Of the consulting engineers, it was Mr. Ferguson with whom we mostly came in contact, and he visited the site fairly frequently. They also had a site staff, in charge of the resident engineer, Mr. A. J. Pringle. His office was on the Connel section, and he had on each section one or more assistant engineers, and also at least one inspector to supervise the quality of the work.

Much of the work requiring closest inspection was concrete or masonry, and it was usually considered that a mason made the best inspector, or failing him a bricklayer.

The relations between the engineer's and contractor's staffs were reasonably good. It was inevitable that differences should arise in connection with the work, but with a little tact and fair-mindedness these differences could be kept from becoming personal. Certainly in the junior ranks, we remained on the best of terms. The resident engineer's assistants on the Ballachulish section were housed in a bungalow known as the Shelter, and were looked after by a middle-aged housekeeper. The Shelter was only about a mile from my home, and was a frequent port of call. One member of the staff called McLean had a phonograph with half a dozen very good musical records in the form of cylinders. We got to know these extremely well.

Among the navvies, however, even when there was no desire to scamp their work, there was a traditional feeling that the inspector was fair game, a feeling such as might be held by a sporting poacher towards a gamekeeper who was but trying to do his duty. Jimmy O'Neill was one of the gangers, a man with a walrus moustache, puffy eyes and a mischievous twinkle that boded ill for troublesome inspectors. With his gang of fellow Irishmen he tackled most jobs, but concrete was his speciality.

'Did ye see Mr. Richards?' he asked one day. (Ben Richards was the inspector, a bricklayer by trade, and not a bad sort.)

'He's very pleased with me this mornin'.'

'How's that?'

'Well, last week when we were concratin' he came along an' says he, "There was a bit of frost in the air last night, Jimmy. Who told ye to concrate?" I didn't say nothin', but I went up to the bit of wet rag I always have hangin' near the board in this kind of weather. When it gets hard I stop mixin'. It was quite soft, an' he had to agree there was no reason to stop me. But he had brought with him a tin an' he took away the fill of it of the wet concrate. I watched him while he went off over the hill an' I saw the hole in the wall he hid it in. As soon as he was out of sight I sent the nipper to fetch it. We emptied out what was in it an' filled it with some rale good stuff. When he found it this mornin' an' saw the way it was settin' he couldn't hardly believe his eyes.'

4

The Workshops

WHEN I JOINED the staff there was as yet no office on the Ballachulish section. Mr. Wilson lived with the Boss (who had taken over a large house for himself and his family) and, like the rest of the staff, did his paper work at home. In the meantime, when not working outside with Mr. Rose, my headquarters for the next few months were the small group of workshops and stores at Kentallen. The workshops consisted of an old stone-built smithy and a wooden joiners' shop that had been built alongside, and was just about big enough for two joiners to work in without getting in each other's way. The carpenter or joiner was not necessarily a trained man, for a handy man was more adaptable, and, therefore, could often be more useful on a construction job than a specialist.

Normally the works' smithy was concerned with the routine sharpening and tempering of tools from the excavation squads—rock drills, picks and pinch bars, as well as the hundred-and-one other jobs of forging and welding that came in from time to time. But here a rather special line was added, for the tools from the black-granite quarry, to which reference is made in a later chapter, were also dealt with. The stone was excavated in large blocks by the quarriers, cut up into rough approximate forms by cutters, and dressed by hewers to the required shapes and sizes. This called for the making and servicing of the special tools required by these men—hand drills with plugs and feathers for the cutters, and chisels, punches (locally called 'clurers') and other dressings tools used by the hewers. These quarry tools took up a large part of the blacksmith's time. Perhaps I should here explain the 'plugs and feathers' mentioned above, as they filled a very important and interesting part in the preparation of the stone. The plug was a small steel wedge, about four inches long, forged out of a bar about $\frac{3}{4}$-in. square. The feather was made from half-round steel about $\frac{1}{2}$-in. wide and 3 in. long, worked to a taper by the smith and the tip bent back. The cutter drilled a row of small holes in the stone along the line he wished to cut, and in each he placed a plug, with a feather, small end up, on each side of it to provide smooth surfaces for the plug to slide. He then tapped on each plug in turn with a hand hammer, or if necessary a heavier two-handed hammer, over and over again till the stone split in two like a coconut. Blocks of granite, man-high, could be cut in this way.

The tempering of the tools by the blacksmith had to be carefully done, in a manner suited to the purpose for which the tool was used; if made too hard the tips were brittle and liable to break off, if too soft they burred up quickly and lost their edge.

When the tool had been sharpened by hammering on the anvil it was usually allowed to cool. Then the end was reheated to a bright red, and the tip chilled in a tub of cold water. The scale was then quickly removed from one side with a bit of pumice stone or other abrasive, and the smith watched while the residual heat in the steel pushed a band of colour towards the tip, a band that varied from light straw colour, which gave the hardest temper, through darker straws to purples, and finally to shades of blue, which gave a point or edge too soft for the general run of excavators' or masons' tools. The smith knew by experience what colour suited the purpose of each tool. When the shade he wanted reached the tip, the picks, drills and other large tools were completely quenched in the tub, and then thrown on the floor or outside, to be collected by the nipper from the gang that would use them. But the punches, chisels and other small tools of the workers in stone required more careful treatment. Instead of the final quenching, they were stood on end in a box with a bare quarter of an inch of water in the bottom, and there left until they had completely cooled off.

The 'nipper' who brought the tools from the quarry was old Allan Dubh (Black Allan), about eighty years of age, with raven black hair and side whiskers. He plodded along the quarter mile or so between quarry and smithy with his wheelbarrow, stopping when he felt like it to rest on the barrow and chat with passers-by. The smithy was his club. Here, when awaiting his tools to be sharpened he sat and listened to the club gossip, occasionally throwing in a telling word. His mother tongue was Gaelic, and his use of English was scanty, but his mind was alert and his converse flavoured with a pawky sense of humour. His wage would be less than that of a labourer, but he was happy. Years after, when the standard wage came into being, my mind sprang at once to old Allan and his like, who would be the first to lose their jobs, and much of their interest in life, when younger men could be had for the same cost.

Sandy McLean had charge of the store—tools, cement, timber, steel and all the rest of it. He was a sturdy and serious type of man, of middle height, with a neatly pointed beard. At one time he had been a quarryman, but in spite of a fine physique he had some years before been struck down by tuberculosis, that deadly scourge of the Western Highlands. In the Glasgow hospital where he was sent for treatment the professor brought his students around and lectured to them on Sandy's well-developed torso, but in the end they had to send him out incurable, as far as the hospital was concerned. He went home again, and spent much of his time out on the hillside in a long chair when the weather allowed him, resting and breathing the pure Highland air, while his wife worked indomitably to keep the home together. In time they won the fight, and Sandy was now a healed man, able to do work less strenuous than he had done before, but no less useful. He was well read and thoughtful, and what with his books and his wide practical experience, he was an interesting and informative man to listen to.

The smithy was a focal point at mid-day for any man who happened to be working in the vicinity. Here they could boil their drums of tea at the forge, eat their dinner in shelter and swap yarns and news while the smith was having his own meal at his nearby lodgings. At other times of the day men came in with tools to sharpen or special jobs for the smith, and sometimes had to hang around till the work was done, adding their quota of gossip to the general stream.

'Did ye hear what they done to old Johnnie McAdam on Saturday night?' (McAdam was a well-known character in the district, and had a beard that reached halfway to his waist.) 'Some of the boys found him dead drunk in the ditch and cut off the one side of his whiskers. He's had to cut off the other side to match.'

'Aye, and they say he knew fine all the time who was doin' it but couldn't move a finger.'

'Queer, the way the drink takes some folks different. Me, after I've had three or four I don't know where I am till mornin', but my legs is the last things to let me down.'

Perhaps another aspect of this queerness was in the mind of the kindly fellow who, noticing that I was snuffling from a heavy cold on a damp and chilly day, gave me the benefit of his wide experience. 'If I was you I would get four gills of rum inside o' me and go and lie down on the turnpike road.'

But amidst a welter of idle talk a word was sometimes spoken that was arresting:

'Did you ever come across Bob Fletcher?' one asked of his neighbour.

'I've heard his name. What did he do? Wasn't he a platelayer or something, or did he drive a loco?'

'Everything. Bob used to reckon he could tackle anything inside of a railway fence, and he could an' all.'

Anything inside a railway fence? But wasn't that in a different sense the job of the civil engineer? If building railways happened to be his line, wasn't he responsible for all the work inside the fence, including the fence itself, and if he did his job properly, he must needs know a great deal about that work. It would not be expected of him that he should be able to perform each skill as well as the man whose job it was, but at least he should know *how* it was done, and whether or not it was done properly. And if he knew that he would, at least, not lay himself open to the scornful jibe I once heard levelled at a man of book-learning and little practical experience: 'Yon man knows nothin' but what's in the specification.'

Thus early the need for the engineer to have wide practical

knowledge came home to me, and the vision stayed. Was this reaching for the moon? It is true that while at the turn of the century life was a more simple affair, there has since been such a great advance in scientific research in regions too wide for the engineer to cover, that he is now obliged to share his responsibility with others. Where, however, within the compass of his own responsibility he must for practical reasons delegate his authority to subordinate or specialist, the choice of these is his concern, and he cannot absolve himself of his overall responsibility for their actions.

I have never had cause to regret these early aspirations, least perhaps when in odd corners of the earth, I have been confronted with willing workers, ignorant of modern ways but willing to be taught, and the specialist was not there to teach them.

Here then was a chance to put principles into practice, for there were lots of useful things to be learned around the workshops. Sometimes I watched the joiners at work or helped them put together a wheelbarrow or shaft a few tools. Amateur helpers were not usually popular in a blacksmith's shop, but Johnny McRae was a tolerant sort of chap and let me try things when he wasn't too pressed for work. His striker was at first an odd-looking man called McCandy. He had a long black beard, large disorderly feet and a squint. If he had been hammered out straight, he would, I think, have measured well over six feet, but he shambled along roughly in the shape of a figure 'S'. He had some queer tricks, and once to impress me he took a red-hot hand drill from the fire, licked it and put it back. I never learned how he did it. What I liked about him was that he never minded handing over his forehammer to me. Once, when I made a bad shot and missed the steel I was striking, the smith burst out laughing and shoved it back in the fire again.

'That's no' as bad as the fellow I heard about the other day,' he said. 'The smiddy was at the side of the loch the same as this one, and the tide was in. The striker wasn't much of a hand, and when he took a side swipe at something the smith was cutting on the floor, he missed the thing completely and the hammer flew out of his hand and landed in the loch. The smith took a turn to the door and looked at the rings on the water where the hammer had gone. "Well," says he, "I've seen some strikers before that missed the anvil now and again, but you're the first I've come across that missed the face of the earth!".'

However, I soon got familiar with the striker's work, and could fill a gap when McCandy failed and I happened to be free. Once, when there was a rush on at the smithy and the striker was absent, I swung the ten-pound forehammer till after midnight before trudging home through the quiet of the night to my bed.

From there to the other side of the anvil was but a step, and before very long it happened that Johnny the smith, after starting the day with a very bad head, went home and was not seen again that day. The quarry was crying out for tools, and I had no other commitments, so I took off my coat and reached for the blacksmith's apron. I was relieved to find in due course that old Allan brought back no recriminations from the quarrymaster.

There was no lack of other odd jobs for the new pupil, such as trudging miles with Sandy the storekeeper to take stock of iron fencing materials that had been dumped in lots along the route some time before and were now half-buried in growing grass, or checking a cargo of wooden posts and rails that were being shipped in the old puffer to another part of the line. This latter nearly had me beat, as the stuff was being passed down into the hold by two chains of men, one handling the posts and the other the rails. However, I managed to get it under control by giving my hands the notebook and pencil to put a tick down automatically as each rail passed them, while my mind concentrated on counting the posts. One day it would be going along with a new carpenter, unused to this kind of work, and passing on to him the but lately acquired knowledge of how to erect the centring for a concrete bridge; another day it would be a trip to Oban by steamer to collect from another messenger a box of a hundred detonators, which could easily go into the pocket, but if dropped on the deck could just as easily remove all trace of whoever it was who had been so unfortunate as to drop them.

5

Office and Field

THE WINTER DAYS shortened quickly, and lengthened again with seeming slowness at the turn of the year. As more men drifted on to the site, fresh gangs were started, and new cuttings opened, gradually lengthening the field of operations along the section. The new office was finished early in the year, a two-roomed affair, one room for the engineers and the other for the clerical staff—cashier, clerk and timekeeper. This was a great improvement. True, it lengthened my daily trudge morning and evening to five miles, but this was no great hardship unless the weather was foul. The walk was lightened at times by the company of a fellow traveller. On a rare occasion it might be Canon McKenzie, a hard-working little man who took his local services on the Sunday, and on the Monday morning walked to Ballachulish Ferry and crossed to Onich to take some service there for his bishop. He carried a fund of odd and interesting bits of local intelligence. Near Kentallen one day he paused and pointed across Loch Linnhe to where Glen Tarbert ran straight through the mountains to Loch Sunart in the west.

'It will be fair today,' he said. 'We call that the Golden Valley. If you can see clear through to the horizon, it means that good weather is on the way.'

Later on I got a second-hand bicycle, which made things easier and saved some shoe-leather. But that had its limitations, for often one's work made it necessary to walk along the line. The roads also left much to be desired. Once a year they were given a coat of 2-in. stone, broken by hand, and this was left for the iron-shod traffic to roll in. There was no roller. Now and again the roadman moved along the edges throwing back into the centre any stones that had been flicked out by the traffic, and it is only fair to say that nearly always there was a smooth, narrow margin along the edges where a bicycle could run.

I must here point out that, while the centre line of the railway had already been set out by the original surveyors, it was the contractor's responsibility to do all further setting out required during construction. The resident engineer's assistants rather envied us this experience, and when there was something of special interest to be set out we occasionally allowed them to come along and give us a hand.

The longer days took Mr. Rose and myself further afield, setting out and levelling for bridges, road diversions and other works, so that all should be in readiness before the gangs moved in. If the distance from the office was long we could usually arrange for level, theodolite or other gear to be sent in advance: if not, we carried them. There are pleasant memories of sitting out on the hillside while we ate our sandwiches, with a wide stretch of sea and mountain before us, the only sign of life being a few sheep grazing nearby, and on the loch perhaps one of MacBrayne's paddle steamers passing far out in stately grace, or a distant smudge that meant a plebeian puffer chugging along around the coast to bring its cargo of coal to some lonely beach. Mr. Rose, an artist from his inner soul to his fingertips, would have his pencil out to sketch with a few deft strokes in the back of his notebook or on some scrap of paper whatever caught his fancy, and encourage his inadequate pupil to follow him along the artistic path.

Another memory that sticks in the mind is of a hot summer's day when we were doing some survey or setting-out work in the grounds behind Craigrannoch House. Dusty and sweating in the windless air, we were about to finish and call it a day, when a gracious lady moved towards us through the rhododendrons, carried us indoors to the cool comfort of her drawing-room and charmed away our weariness with the hospitality of her tea table.

Fortunate it is for us that as time passes it is memories of the halcyon days that stay with us, and we are apt to forget the storms and the rough places on the road, till some incident is recalled that reminds us, such as of going out on a fine-looking morning without a coat, getting drenched, and then standing in front of the blacksmith's fire, front and back alternately, till the steam stopped rising.

Normally we were prepared for bad weather, and what with stout ankle boots, leather leggings, lightweight double oilskins and sou'westers, we could get through to the end of the day pretty dry, if the wind was not too high. But if half a gale was blowing on top of the rain or sleet, nothing could stop the wet from getting through our defences.

It was on one such wild, wet day that we met one of the resident engineer's assistants heading into the driving rain. He turned his back to the weather for a moment to give us a bit of topical news. He had just heard that the rainfall for the previous twelve months had been recorded as 110 inches, which was higher than normal. I do not think it was an official record, but was measured by an enterprising local worthy who kept a rain gauge for his own satisfaction. But if anything approaching a fathom and a half of water fell upon us from the heavens in the course of the year, it would not be surprising if we sometimes did get wet.

Checking the cuttings was a regular task for the section engineer. The means to ensure that these and the embankments were kept true to line and level were simple. Before a cutting was started the section engineer gave the ganger his centre line and a formation level. He would also mark off for some way ahead points at which the slope of the cutting—earth or rock as the case might be—would strike the surface. The ganger would string a line between these points and cut a 'locksplit' or nick in the turf to mark the limit of his excavation. He could then strip any suitable top soil and cast it aside clear of the work for future use. As soon as the cutting was far enough advanced, the engineer would give him two pegs some distance apart at formation level. Every ganger was provided with a set of three crossheads or boning rods, which were simply planed pieces of narrow board, exactly three feet long, with a short crosspiece on the top, painted white or black for clear sighting. Two of these, one white and one black, were held on the pegs, and the ganger, going ahead with the third and sighting across the top could tell to a fraction of an inch how his cutting was going. While checking of the work by the section engineer was a matter of routine, if the ganger thought a peg had been disturbed or his excavation was getting too far ahead, he asked the engineer for a special check.

The centre-line pegs as originally set out were usually found undisturbed, and as the work approached them the engineer transferred the numbered index peg to the side, preferably to a distance divisible by five feet, so that he could record its distance by a nick in the front of the peg for each ten feet, and one in the back for five. This gave a good enough base for checking the work until the final setting out for the permanent way. For the embankments, double-headed crossheads were erected ahead of the tip, the lower at formation level, and the other three feet higher, for sighting purposes.

Mr. Rose went off in due course for a week's holiday. Left to myself, I lost no time in getting out on the job with the levelling instrument and a labourer to hold the staff, checking all the cuttings!

Another routine task was the monthly measurement. Towards the end of each month an estimate had to be made of the work done up to the 25th, so that payment on account could be made to the contractor. In fine weather it was pleasant to walk down the line and make a record of progress, but not so nice when the weather was rough. Most outside work could be postponed in bad weather till things improved; not so the measurement. Rain, hail or snow, we had to get on with it, and that might mean a walk of a dozen miles or so.

For the next two or three days it was all hands—Wilson, Rose and myself—to the job of running out the quantities for the hundreds of items that made up the measurement, and then the whole thing had to be written out by hand in fair: the typewriter had not yet barged its way into popularity. If, as sometimes happened, we were working late, Mr. Wilson would perhaps give me dinner. It might be ten or eleven before we packed up, and then the five-mile walk home to clear away the cobwebs.

When the contract started there must have been some attempt made to agree the quantities month by month with the staff of the resident engineer—a normal procedure. If so, it had been abandoned, and now each party got out their own measurement. Payment would only be made on the resident engineer's certificate, and any differences that existed between that and the contractor's statement (and there were many) were carried forward to be dealt with as claims at the end of the contract, unless some agreement was come to in the meantime.

There was another regular measurement, made only by the contractor, to keep a constant check on the cost of the work. For every four-week period the timekeeper had to produce a statement, known as the Slump Time Abstract, showing the labour cost against each item. This was an approximation, and he was allowed an error of two pounds between his abstract and the sum of the two fortnightly paysheets. Extra columns were provided for the section engineer, who filled in against each item the quantity of work done, the schedule price and actual cost, and the total earned for the period. As hand labour was responsible for a very large proportion of the total cost, the contractor could see at a glance how his contract was faring, and many a sharp rejoinder came from head office, demanding an explanation when costs appeared to be too high.

Sometimes a job was done by piecework, and that meant an extra measurement to be carried out by the hard-working section engineer at the end of each fortnight. It might be that a gang of a few men from the same part of the country would get together to take on a job, and share out the results among them on pay-day. Or one man of a more ambitious type would sub-contract the work himself and hire such labour as would trust him for their wages when pay-day came round. Or again, a single man with perhaps a mate would 'sub' a small job and hope to make something more of it than an ordinary day's wage.

One of the last type I remember was a man, Dan Smith, who offered to take on a soft cutting at the rate of fivepence a cubic yard. It was a low price which meant that he and anyone with him would each have to move at least ten cubic yards a day to earn even a normal working wage. But the cutting was an ideal one, fine, soft sand that required practically no picking, just shovelling into the barrow and wheeling to the tip. As the cutting had just been started, the lead was at first negligible, and the results on the first pay-day were quite satisfactory. As the distance from cut to fill lengthened, however, the output went down. He was a decent middle-aged man and he and his mate worked hard. On the second pay-day his packet was a good deal less, and he asked rather diffidently if we could not increase his rate a bit. I had to tell him that, without mentioning it, we had already raised his rate to sevenpence, for we could see he was doing a good day's work.

These little contracts seldom lasted long; the question of measurement was always a stumbling-block to the unlettered worker. Straightforward one-dimension jobs such as plate-laying and ditching were preferred. I was told of one case where a small gang of Irish labourers had taken on at a piecework rate the excavation of some wall foundations on a building contract. On the first pay-day they were evidently greatly disappointed with the takings, and after some discussion among themselves they came back and asked my friend, the quantity surveyor, would he mind checking up again and seeing if he hadn't made a mistake? He did so, but there was no mistake. They went into a huddle again, and then one bright lad had a brainwave.

'Say,' he said, 'How many feet have ye taken in yer cube yard?'

'Twenty-seven,' said the measurer.

'Ah! No wonder it's not comin' right. We was reckonin' on nine!'

6

The Walking Ganger

THE WALKING GANGER on the Ballachulish section was a man called Addison, short, bearded, impetuous, bursting with explosive energy and somewhat fierce of aspect, but kindly inside when you got to know him. As a youngster he and the Boss had known each other and they were both of an age. His father, who worked for the firm, had one day found them fighting. Seizing his son, he threw him over a wall, to the imminent risk of his neck. The first earning job of the boy Addison was sitting on the rump of a trace horse, helping heavy-laden lorries up some of the steeper hills on city streets. Horses were still his first love, and it was a happy arrangement that when he was given the farm-house at Lagnaha to live in, the stables were at his elbow, where most of the firm's horses on the section were housed. He was up at five every morning, seeing that his horsemen were on the spot, their charges properly attended to and out on the road in time for the start of their work. A faithful servant himself, he looked for faithful service from those under him. Not a link or a buckle escaped his eye.

Trotting down the road in the trap one day and talking as he drove, his eye automatically scanned a led horse that was approaching. Then he reined in suddenly with a roar, 'Woho! Look at your horse-cover, man, look at it! Don't ye know which end goes foremost? Some of you fellas need to have a photty of the horse painted on the dazzened cover to tell ye the front from the backside.' His wrath expressed itself in the waving whip. 'If I ever find ye doin' that again, I'll—I'll——' Then his eye fell from the offending cover to the small, one-eyed culprit, cowering under the threatened onslaught. Then the gale dropped suddenly to a gentle breeze. 'I'll cut yer heid aff! Gerrup, Cherry!' And on we trotted again.

It was never dull going down the line with Alick Addison. Opposite the post office a man was standing counting his change. He had recently taken on one of the earth cuttings on piecework.

'Well, Crawford, how are ye gettin' along?' says Addison.

'Not so well at all. I'm takin' the day off to give ma back a rest. That ground of yours, man, is hard, as hard as the duvvel.'

Addison's eyes twinkled. 'What? They tell me he's saft.'

'Ah, well, you'll have to change your ways or you'll find oot your mistake!'

As we left Crawford to his holiday, apropos of nothing, 'I'm forty the day,' said Addison, then with a sidelong challenge in his eye, 'Ye wouldn't think it to look at me?'

I glanced at his rugged, bearded face, made some non-committal murmur, and wished him many happy returns.

Down the road a local man was coming with a few pieces of broken board on his shoulder. Alick knew him, I think.

'Woho! Where did ye get that?'

'They were lying near the road.'

'Who did ye ask for them?'

'Nobody. I wanted some bits like that and I didn't think these were any use to anybody.'

'Well,' said Addison quietly, 'ye can take them, but next time ye find something that's nae use tae anybody just ask for it. What's worth liftin' is worth askin' for.'

Going along the road one day near the office, where the line branched off from near the highway and disappeared up the slope into the wood, I was arrested by an approaching sound of crashing among the trees. Suddenly, a black man burst from the undergrowth, dashed across the road and down on to the fore-shore. A few yards behind him came the walking ganger, not walking now but at full gallop. The sight of a twelve-pointer stag would have been less startling, for at that time the practice had not yet begun of immigrants from our far-flung empire flocking into the over-populated little island that was its heart, and a dark gentleman in the Highlands was a more rare phenomenon than the aurora borealis. This one, seeing Loch Leven in front of him, came to a halt and picked up a stone about

the size of a well-grown orange. Addison went no further than
the road and contented himself with hurling from there a few
final comments after the fugitive. The trouble arose, I learned,
from his giving an order to the man and getting an impudent
reply, a thing he did not take to at all kindly. This was the first,
and as far as I remember, the only foreigner I saw employed on
the works.

It sometimes happens that a kind of malaise spreads through a
job, for no apparent reason, and nothing seems to go right. I
knew an engineer who took over as agent a construction contract
that had not been prospering. His first action was to close down
the work for a fortnight. When he started up again he did so
with a clean sheet.

At the southern end of the Ballachulish section, where a few
scattered gangs were working, things were not going well.
Perhaps they were too far from the busy centre of things and were
getting stale. The walking ganger did not know what was wrong,
but he warned the Boss in the office one day that if things did not
improve, he would sack every man at that end of the job. A
couple of days later I was on my way there to do a bit of measuring when I met two or three men whose faces seemed familiar,
trampling listlessly down the road; then some more, until I
finally realised that all the gangs at that end were on the move.
Last of all came Addison, alone, weary and with his voice worn
to a whisper. He had not known what was wrong, but his
instinct told him the remedy. The men, if they wished, could get
work on other parts of the job, and when new gangs were started
a cathartic wind would have blown through and cleared the air.

Ben Richards, the inspector, and Alick Addison were in daily
contact on the work. They were both about the same height, but
seemed to have difficulty in accepting the fact. If you came across
Addison going his rounds, he might well greet you with the
question, referring to the inspector: 'Have ye seen the wee
fella?' (Whether for the purpose of contact or evasion would
depend on the circumstances.) Further on you might run into
Richards and be greeted with the query, referring to Addison:
'Have ye seen the wee fella?' As was natural, they occasionally

had disagreements, but on the whole they got on as well together as could be expected, considering that their respective functions, though not necessarily antagonistic, were liable at times to clash. It was Addison's job to carry out the work efficiently and economically. It was the inspector's business, among other things affecting the quality of the work, to see that the economy was not overdone.

Addison's knowledge of reading and writing was elementary, but on a Saturday afternoon he would sometimes sit in his shirtsleeves and patiently browse over the pages of the daily paper. And on Sunday he might sometimes be seen, dressed up soberly in his best, wending his way with his gentle and capable wife and two small sons towards the Scots kirk, his weekday vigour chastened by the Sabbath calm.

7

Labour

THE LABOURERS WHO worked up and down the line were loosely classified as navvies, but the name calls for some discrimination. It was originally derived from 'navigators', those men who in the eighteenth and early nineteenth centuries laboured on the building of the canals of England, or 'navigations' as they were then called. When the navvies turned from the building of canals to railways and other public works they brought with them their name and many of their characteristics.

A large proportion of the railway navvies came from Ireland, but in time they came from many other parts of the country as well. It was inevitable that when a new work was started, it attracted labour from the surrounding districts, from towns and villages and from the land. Some of these newcomers might stay for part of the year and return home when the seasonal demands of farm or croft or fishing called them. Others might stay till the end of the job, but when it was finished they had to move on and search for other work. The life tended to make them nomadic, and to sever home ties.

The authentic navvy was a nomad. He might stick to his job for a week or a year, but whenever the urge came he was off down the road. In some things he was sensitive. You could tell him how you wanted the job done, and he would do his best to do it your way, but if you started to show him, you had to be careful. 'Take the tool out of a man's hand!' That was the last indignity, and good men have walked down the road just for that. Or again it might be on a Monday morning when all of his world felt grim and his nerves were on edge, that a hasty word from ganger or walking ganger would touch off the spark, and the man would down the tool he was using and reach for his jacket. See him as he stumped away towards his next job, which might be another section of the line or fifty miles away. His work-worn dress was unmistakable, almost a uniform—the peaked cap, ample coat and waistcoat with ample pockets, and corduroy trousers held below the knees with leather straps—'yorks' he called them. If he happened to be the ganger he might give his men the 'Gee-ho!' to down tools and follow him. In the course of the contract he might return once and again, for there were no hard feelings on either side.

The navvy lived a hard life, but it did not seem to break his spirit. He was the most independent man on earth, and he had no use for trade unions. Rough and dissipated he might be; he had a code of his own, and he was loyal and charitable to his mates. I was standing on the quay one day, watching the unloading of materials from a small coastal craft, when I noticed a ganger who had left his job two or three days before come hurrying through among the men. He spoke hardly a word, nudged the elbow of one man and looked dumbly at another; and hell was in his eyes. He was a humourless sort of man, and I don't think that as a ganger he had ever been very popular. A round-faced young chap who was standing beside me reached down into the pocket of his moleskins and passed the ganger a half-day's pay. 'I wouldn't see no man dry,' he muttered with gruff apology.

There were good and bad workmen, as there were good and bad employers. But the navvy had an instinctive loyalty to the man who paid his wages, even if he were a hard taskmaster who did not always measure up to the highest standards. 'If you're working for a man work for him', was the core of his creed. Was this loyalty perhaps akin to that of many primitive peoples, such as the Pathan on the North West Frontier, who might rob his neighbour or his Sahib's neighbour, but would scorn to be a 'traitor to his salt' and steal from his own Sahib?

As was the navvy, so was the navvy ganger, who was but an aristocrat among his fellows. He attained his position by ability and force of personality, and owed little to schooling. It was surprising how often one's best ganger was practically illiterate. Like his men he might today throw up his job and disappear, and a few months hence be back and start working as a labourer, but if he was a good man the eagle eye of the walking ganger would quickly spot him and hale him out to take again the charge of a gang.

It was the ganger's business to engage his men, and he usually had a shrewd eye for character.

'Why did you turn away that man, Jack? I thought you were short-handed.'

'Aye, I'm short-handed, but yon man's bum's too near the grund.'

I wonder what an anthropologist would have made of that.

The men lived in huts provided by the contractor. Each hut was looked after by a woman hut-keeper who kept the place in order. In some huts she also cooked for the men; in others they cooked for themselves on the hotplate. They were tough, these women. They had to be, to hold their own with such a crowd, but the rough tongue that could scourge her charges in language that matched their own often concealed a warm heart, for which many a poor chap who was down on his luck had cause to be thankful. A male relative of the hut-keeper, who was usually also a ganger, acted as 'deputy' and dealt when necessary with rowdy customers, who were too much for even the hut-keeper.

There was little comfort, especially when the weather was bad. If the rain began after the men had started work they would often work steadily on till they were thoroughly wet, and then go trudging home to hut or lodgings. Perhaps by that time the rain was clearing, but they were finished for the day.

The men worked a ten-hour day in summer, from 7 a.m. till 5.30 p.m., with a half-hour break for dinner at midday, and from 7 till 1 on Saturday, giving them a 56-hour week. Winter hours were shorter, and were governed by the length of daylight. 'Dinner' consisted of whatever food the men had brought with them—bread, meat and cheese. If a man was near the bottom of his purse he might make do with bread and jam—'Dundee beef' he called it—an allusion to one of the industries for which Dundee was noted. All was washed down with a mug of hot tea.

An hour or so before noon the nipper would fill a bucket with water and hang it over a fire, usually in the open, unless a blacksmith's fire was handy and not too busy. Then a few minutes before the break he would go round the men, collecting from each his little tin of tea and sugar—a tin that had probably started its useful life as a container of Mr. Colman's mustard. These the nipper emptied into the boiling water, and a cup of cold water would likely follow. If you asked him what the cold water was for he might reply that it was to 'tempture' the tea, the tempering no doubt consisting in settling the leaves to the bottom.

The ganger would look at his watch and shout, 'Drum up, boys!'

Wages were paid once a fortnight on the Saturday. The fortnight ended on the previous Thursday, which left the men with two days 'lying time'. This gave the timekeeper time to make up his paysheet and the cashier to put the wages up in pay envelopes and check his balance. The envelopes were left ungummed till the check was made, so that any discrepancy could easily be tracked down. On Saturday morning cashier and timekeeper drove round the works together and paid the men.

The rate of pay was 5*d*. an hour for labourers, for the actual time worked. For gangers it was 5*s*. 6*d*. or 6*s*. a day, paid upstanding for six days a week. Little overtime was worked and the hourly rate was the same as for daytime.

Long Riley was a quiet, reliable sort of man of the upper class of ganger, which meant that he earned thirty-six shillings a week. I asked him once how he managed to spend it all. He assured me he was able to get rid of it all right, but he didn't seem to think the question in the least frivolous.

When a man arrived 'on tramp' and started work his funds were usually at a low ebb, and he drew a 3*s*. sub ticket from the timekeeper on his first day. He might do the same thing daily for the next few days, but after that he was expected to live a less hand-to-mouth existence, and would perhaps 'sub' only twice a week or less. Most of these gentlemen of the road continued to draw sub on the odd Saturday, and many of them also on the pay day, against their two days' lying time. The sub tickets were cashed by the grocer, and in some cases he drove round the works in his van to make it easier for the men to get their cash and buy their 'Tommy' at the same time.

On this question of tramping the road from job to job, I asked Jimmy O'Neill one day:

'How far do you go in a day when you're on tramp?'

He scratched his ear before replying, and the corners of his eyes wrinkled a bit as something tickled his memory.

'Is it me?' he said, 'I'm not often on the tramp. But it differs. It depends on what's before ye and what's after ye. I once knew a man called Pete MacCarthy—Bully MacCarthy, they called him. He was as big as an elephant and twice as nasty, and the more liquor he got inside of him the uglier he was. A murtherous brute. He would fight with his own shadow, and I always tried to keep out of his way. But him and me got into an argument one Saturday afternoon that didn't do me any good. I was lucky to finish up with nothin' worse than a black eye, and I decided it was time for me to be movin'. That evenin' I went down to the burn and greased me feet all over with soft soap. Then I put on me sox and soaked them well. It keeps yer feet from blisterin'. When I got back to the hut there of all things was MacCarthy, spread out on the floor and drunk as a lord. I had on me heaviest boots with the biggest nails in them (me only pair if it comes to that), and I just walked all over him the way he was lyin'. Then I grabbed what belongin's I had and went fast for the turnpike road. When I stopped walkin' I was eighty miles away. That was me longest tramp.'

I have no doubt of Jimmy's ability to stretch a point for artistic effect, but in this case there was an obvious urge to place as many miles as possible behind him before the torpid Bully regained consciousness.

There was a Navvy Mission Society, started away back in the eighteen-seventies to help these wandering workers. The Society published a quarterly letter, and this, in addition to trying to cater for the moral welfare of the men, also gave them useful information of a more mundane sort. There were lists of public works under construction, where a man might get a job, and there were notices of men killed or injured in accidents. Enquiries were published for any who were missing, and scathing condemnation for those who had defrauded their mates or their landladies.

'Will Bill Brown "Pincher" communicate with his wife, who is in need of monetary assistance.'

'Joe (Shorty) Sykes has sloped his landlady in Maverick Lane, Glasgow, owing her a lot for food and lodging. Shame on such men. Landladies, beware.'

On some contracts a navvy missioner was resident on the job. I recall meeting the missioner only once, and if he resided anywhere on this contract it must have been at the southern end of the work before I moved there.

From the coasts and glens of the Highlands there came a different type of labour to work on the line. The Strome Ferry Railway had recently been finished, and many of the men from the surrounding districts who had worked on its construction now came to us. There they had learned many new skills, and these, added to their own native crafts, acquired on croft or boat, helped to make them useful members of the construction crew. There were others, working away from home for the first time, who came dressed in homespun Harris tweeds, with the aura of peat reek still hanging around them. Some were singularly unfamiliar with the use of even pick and shovel, to say nothing of the more complicated tools and plant, but they were big, strong fellows and quick to learn.

These Highland workers represented not so much a class, as a section of the community to which they belonged. The sober, responsible man whose qualities of leadership had made of him an elder in the kirk, now became a ganger. His neighbour, not perhaps so sober or responsible, but with the necessary drive and ability, also found his place in charge of a gang.

There was one ganger whose surname I have forgotten, but who was commonly known by the name of Holy Wullie. A first glance at his face, which was of a fine ruddy colour, might raise a doubt as to whether the name had been given him in satire. But no, on better acquaintance the name proved authentic and the colour deceptive, for Wullie was a sober man and had profound religious convictions, to which he faithfully adhered. He was crossing in the ferry to the church in Onich on one peaceful Sabbath morning in the company of the office clerk and a local builder, who was also a ruling elder of the kirk. The sea was calm, and the only sounds that broke the silence were the splash of the oars and the rattle of the rowlocks. But presently the elder, wishing to make a friendly advance, asked him in the Gaelic: 'How are you getting along with the Duaig these days, William?' The Duaig was a steep, awkward rock bluff where Wullie's gang were blasting out a road diversion. There was no reply, and the elder, thinking his question had not been heard, after a little repeated it. There was a brief pause, and then came the answer, quiet but devastating: 'There are six days in the week for talking about the affairs of this world.'

Further along the line, and spread over the two southern sections, there were four energetic brothers, each in charge of his gang. For some reason they had got together and agreed to forgo the bottle, which had evidently become something of a snare. Be it borne in mind that the Celtic temperament is inclined to extremes, and less to the moderation that is accredited to the Anglo-Saxon. It is all or nothing, strictly sober or blow the roof off.

In due course three of the brothers were disturbed to learn through the grapevine that the fourth had fallen by the way. They could not leave their work in mid-week, but on the first Saturday afternoon they converged on the erring brother to persuade him to return to the path of total abstinence. Something seems, however, to have gone wrong with the conference, for later in the evening it was regrettably reported that all four brothers were seen standing back-to-back in the roadway at Portnacroish and challenging the four quarters of the land to come and do battle with them.

There were lots of Lowland Scots on the work, but not many Englishmen. Alick Addison, himself a Lowlander, had a high regard for the English navvy. We were walking down the line one day and the name of a ganger called Pincher Ross cropped up.

'What is a pincher anyhow?' I asked. 'There seem to be half a dozen men called Pincher on the job.'

'An Englishman.'

'But Ross isn't an Englishman.'

'No, he's not, but he likes to speak a bit la-de-da at times— putting it on, ye know.' He was quiet for a bit, his mind turned back on a new train. 'Have ye ever worked in England? No, well, of course, down on the job at Pateley Bridge we had a lot of English—good fellas, worked steady and always filled up the barra. These chaps,' he waved a hand vaguely towards what I assumed was meant to be the Celtic hinderland, 'they're fine for a push if ye're in a hurry. But if ye want a man that'll keep on steady all day at the same speed, ay an' with a full barra all the time, ye can't beat the English navvy.'

There were many other bits of human flotsam that drifted with the labour current. There was an ex-missionary, not looking very robust, but seemingly keen on his labouring job, there perhaps because his doctor had told him to get work in the open air. There was a sturdy fellow in faded blue, an earring in one ear, and an air of the sea about him, scorning one end of the two-man handbarrow his mates were using and tripping along the gangplank to the shore with the two-hundredweight sack of cement on his shoulder. Now and again a fresh-looking brown-faced lad would appear, very straight in the back, and with tattoo marks on his arms, his looks proclaiming that another man had lately finished with his military service. These unusual types did not as a rule stay long with us, moving on perhaps to find a niche more suited to their talents. But when they did stay, the course of the years would dull the salient colours of their origins, as of their dress, and outwardly at least they would merge into the drab stream of migrant labour.

It might be, however, that a chance encounter would stir to flame the smouldering ashes of by-gone history. Outside the grocer's store one Saturday afternoon a group of men were idling. One of them made a chance remark, and I noticed another turn sharply and look keenly at the speaker. Then he moved over to the man, his eyes still fixed on his face, and said something in a strange tongue. The other stared open-mouthed for a moment and then replied in kind, and immediately there was a burst of recognition, of hand-shaking, and palm-spitting and hand-shaking again. From words they dropped it appeared that many years before they had soldiered together in the East, and for a brief spell the drab reality of muck and cold rain was forgotten in the memories of hot skies and waving palms.

Railway Workmen's Concerts were organised by the contractor's staff, who unearthed quite a lot of talent—some from among themselves and other workers on the line, including the resident engineer's staff, and some from local people. There were songs, and there was music by piano and banjo. The Boss's daughters danced and sang, and one performer of varied talent who worked on the line alternately played the pipes himself and danced the Highland Fling or the Sailor's Hornpipe to the music of others. Mr. Rose made charcoal sketches to a piano accompaniment, his strokes keeping time to the music and the picture illustrating its theme. Then there was the hefty blacksmith who did his own special strong-man turn. He would sit down on the platform, place his hands on the floor behind him and raise his body till only hands and feet supported it. A wooden shutter was placed resting on his shoulders and knees, and on this two of his mates placed a two-hundredweight anvil, which they then proceeded to flog with heavy hammers. There were good attendances at these concerts, but I doubt if many from the dwellers in the navvies' huts along the line put in an appearance.

8

Rocks

A GEOLOGIST GIVES the name rocks to everything of importance that goes to make up the crust of the earth, from peat to Portland stone, from garden soil to granite. Geologists are full of fascinating lore, and how often, when travelling through interesting country, has one wished that a geologist could have been there as a fellow traveller to explain just how this and that bit of unusual scenery came to be formed that way.

The route of the railway afforded an exceptionally fine geological variety for the railway builders to deal with, and not a few problems.

North of Connel Ferry the line ran for perhaps half a mile over the Achnacree moss with its heavy cover of treacherous peat. The ideal way to treat this would have been to dig out the peat under the railway track and replace it with good reliable filling. But this would have been costly, and the problem was solved by running a low earthen embankment over the surface to carry the line, and a lower bank at each side to act as a blanket to prevent the peat from spewing up under the load of passing trains. When, in due course, the trains did run one could see the line sink visibly and rise again when the train had passed, as if on a rubber foundation. North of Benderloch was a raised beach of pebbles, very convenient and easy to use as ballast, but not so effective for holding the track, as the smooth stones did not bite firmly into the sleepers. Further north a large cutting through gravel was enlarged as a borrowpit, and provided much of the material for banking in this section of the line. Here the only mechanical excavator on the contract was installed, an old steam navvy known as a 'Jubilee'.

The south rail approach to Creagan Bridge was carried on a

high gravel embankment, but there must have been a bed of clay in the level ground on which the bank was tipped, for under the pressure of the new load the adjacent land squeezed seawards, carrying a graceful loop of the public road out into Loch Creran. A new section of road was built and then another, so that at one time three loops of the road could be seen lying one outside the other, giving what one might call a history of the movement. Two miles north of Creagan Bridge the line ran in a cutting through a stretch of moorland, consisting of boulder clay with a surface blanket of peat. It earned for itself the title of Dirty Cutting, and gave us much trouble. We shall hear more of this.

For the next ten miles it was comparatively easy going, with some shale rock, easy to excavate, and with no special headaches or gold mines. Near the farm of Lagnaha the flank of Ben Vair was scarred by a quarry of honey-coloured quartzite. It was locally known as the China Quarry, for large blocks of the stone were roughly squared, lowered down the mountainside by cable railway and sent away to be used in grinding tubs in the pottery industry. This was no concern of ours, but a little further on, above Kentallen Bay the line traversed a scree of the same stuff. It looked an easy quarry for railway ballast, though a bit oversize, but when we had installed a steam-driven crusher to break it down, and saw what it did to the crusher jaws inside of the first week, we realised what the qualities were that made quartzite so useful to the pottery people in dealing with their intractible clays.

Then near the old Kentallen pier the line ran through an outcrop of what the local quarriers called black granite, and which geologists have named kentallenite in honour of the place. This was suitable for dressing, and so the cutting became a quarry and produced quantities of large ashlar blocks for use elsewhere on the line. Beyond Kentallen there was grey granite country, with the busy little quarry of Lettermore as its heart; and finally the line reached its terminus within the encircling quarries of dark blue slate that made the name of Ballachulish so well known among building circles throughout the land.

To the geologist a rock means one thing; to the civil engineer and the public works contractor it means another. For excavation

forms a large part of the work with which they have to deal, and
the classification of the stuff excavated has to be roughly related
to the cost of its removal. Surface excavation is often simply
classed as 'rock' and 'soft', and that was the case here. With the
wide variety of ground that had to be excavated on the line there
was plenty of room for differences of interpretation, but I do not
remember that we had any serious disputes on that score. Many
have tried to lay down clearly a dividing line between rock and
soft. About this time I heard an engineer of wide experience give
a definition of rock that I have not been able to better, and I think
it is worth recording: 'Rock is any material other than earth or
clay, that requires to be quarried or blasted.' The definition had
been put forward by a contractor who in the course of his digging
had struck a seam of coal—a profitable windfall. He claimed that
it was rock and won his case.

There were, of course, anomalies. The contract price for rock
was three times that for soft, and yet the cost of digging out the
'soft' heavy boulder clay could be greater than that of the easily
fractured shale rock.

Boulders found in the soft excavation, if larger than two men
could conveniently handle, were classed as rock. These were
rolled to one side till the inspector came along, when he and the
ganger would agree on the sizes. They were then supposed to be
taken away and dumped in the tip. In one soft cutting where the
proportion of boulders was high, perhaps up to twenty per cent
of the whole, the ganger was a scurvy knave who would have
robbed his own grandmother and took a fiendish delight in
diddling the inspector. His favourite trick was to save the old
boulders and present them for measurement time and again, their
faces all nicely smeared over with a fresh coat of earth, to look
as if they had only that morning for the first time seen the light
of day. When the cutting was nearing completion and we found
from our measurements that the volume of boulders returned
was greater than that of the whole cutting, the section engineer
thought it was time he intervened, and came to a more equitable
agreement with his opposite number.

When a boulder in soft cutting was too big to be manhandled, it was broken up by blasting. This could be done by drilling a small hole to take the charge or by 'plastering', that is, laying the charge on top of the boulder and covering it with clay to exclude the air. The plaster was a handy method when drills were not available, but it took more gelignite to be effective than was needed for charging a drill hole.

In a rock cutting, after a series of shots had been fired, secondary blasting was often necessary to break up the larger pieces, but if the depth of the cutting justified it, a small hand derrick, with a lifting capacity of a ton or so, was usually erected on the top of the cutting for loading up the heavier stuff into the wagons with the minimum amount of further breaking up. From time to time as the cutting advanced the derrick was taken down by the carpenter and re-erected further ahead.

It must be remembered that, ahead of the filling in embankments, all bridges, culverts and other works passing under the line had to be built, so that the earthwork could carry on without any hold-up. Sometimes there was a rush for this, as for instance when the walking ganger announced one day that he would like to switch a gang on to one of these advance works the following morning. The men would have to load up their tools and other gear first thing in the morning on to horse-drawn lorries for transfer to the new site. So we were able to get there an hour ahead of them and had a busy time setting out and putting in a level or two, but the last peg was driven by the time the gear was unloaded.

'Now then, boys, coats off!' from the ganger.

There are one or two laggards, for the morning is chilly.

'Coats off!' roars the ganger again, 'every man that has a shirt on.' There is more haste to comply; no man wants it to be thought that he cannot afford a shirt.

Most of the excavation was done by hand. As a new cutting was opened the muck was barrowed out to form the embankment, till the lead of fifty to a hundred yards became too long. Then flat-bottomed rails were laid for tipping-wagons hauled by a horse. This tipping was quite an art on the part of all concerned, including the horse. When a wagon was full the horse was connected up by a light chain, one end of which had a ring that was placed over the coupling hook in front of the wagon. The other end had a long link that rested similarly on a hook on the horse's swingle tree. The horse, as it hauled, walked alongside the track. When they reached a suitable distance from the bankend, the driver, at a signal from the bankend man, urged the horse on to a lumbering gallop, then at a shout of command and a smack on the rump the horse swung out of the way of the oncoming wagon, while the driver, running alongside, snatched the link from the swingle tree and in one movement swung the chain free from the coupling hook on the wagon. At the tip there was a bumper composed of two or three 'bumpsticks', or sleepers, set on edge transversely one above the other across the track, and curved to take the shock of the wheels. The front of the wagon had a hinged falling door, held up by a catch. The bankend man stood a couple of yards back from the tip with his shovel raised. As the wagon reached him he tripped the catch, the door dropped, the wheels struck the bumper, and if the speed was right the body of the wagon rose, tipped the contents over the end, and fell back empty. If the speed was too great, or the muck too sticky and clung to the sides, it might well be that the wagon would turn right over and roll down the bank, involving salvage operations that caused delay, and the services later of the wagon-fettler to make good the damage. Much depended on the bankend man, and a good one was usually paid a penny an hour over the labour rate, and earned it.

No attempt was made to consolidate the embankments, which were left to settle by natural process in the course of time. Most of them had from one to three years in which to do this, with traffic running over them and helping the work of consolidation.

Later, as the cuttings were worked out one after another and the embankments closed, the length of haul became too great for a horse. A stretch of the formation would then be ballasted, the permanent way laid and a little steam 'pug' or tank engine put on to haul the traffic.

The soft excavation on the Ballachulish section was easy stuff to handle, but between Kentallen and the Ferry there was a lot of granite, some of the cuttings being pretty deep. That set the pace of progress in the area and an early start was made on it.

There was always a fascination in the sight of a rock cutting in full swing, perhaps fifteen to twenty feet deep, with half a dozen sets of drillers strung over the face, the air vibrant with the music of their hammers. The work tended to produce men of fine physique, who handled their seven-pound hammers with an air of easy grace. Their style varied with their background. 'See that new man down below there,' says the ganger, 'he's a miner. Ye can see he's used to workin' in tight places. Look at the way he doesn't raise the hammer above his head, but slips it back over his shoulder.'

As they varied in style so they varied in the philosophies of their calling: 'It's the smartest blow and not the heaviest that cuts the rock.' 'I don't like them hammers with the flat sides. They haven't got no bounce—hang on yer hand the whole blasted day, they do. Gimme a hammer with taperin' sides, and a face about the size of a penny: it comes back to yer shoulder after every blow.'

Each set of drillers consisted of three men—two strikers and one who sat astraddle behind the drill (or jumper as it was more commonly called) held it in his hands and turned it a fraction after each blow. Beside him was a battered tin of water, and from time to time he poured a little into the hole. A twist of grass or rag around the jumper arrested any splash. As the slurry from the powdered stone began to thicken, and turning became difficult, out went the holder's forefinger, a signal for the drillers to stop. He took out the jumper and proceeded to clean out the hole with a slender rod which had a small disc about an inch in diameter formed at right-angles to the end. The jumper itself was of hexagonal steel formed to a stout chisel-shaped cutting edge. As the edge got blunt the jumper was laid aside to be taken to the blacksmith for resharpening, and a slightly longer one taken in its place.

The drills were usually in sets, each drill about six inches longer than its predecessor, depending on the hardness of the rock it had to penetrate—the harder the rock the less penetration achieved before the drill was blunt. The width of the bit also narrowed slightly with each successive length, to allow for the wear on the previous drill and consequent narrowing of the hole as it went down.

It happened sometimes that the tempered cutting end of the drill broke off in the hole, usually due to faulty tempering. The bit must be recovered before drilling could proceed, and for this an ingenious but simple device was used. At one end of a slender steel rod two flat flexible fingers were welded, flaring slightly outwards. Another rod had a ring formed at right-angles to its length. The first rod was pushed down the hole till the fingers passed over the broken bit. Then the ring on the second rod was slipped over the first and pushed down till it gripped the fingers tight against the bit, and the whole was then easily removed. For some reason I could never discover, this device was called a bitch.

From time to time the men changed places, so that each in turn had a change of job. In summer weather the man sitting holding the drill had perhaps the best of it, but on a cold day he was glad to have a trick at the hammer to keep his blood flowing.

The holes would be three to five feet deep, driven vertically or at an angle, depending on the lie of the rock. But later, when some of the Ballachulish quarriers came to work for us they brought with them a style of their own. The tremendous subterranean pressures that originally went to create the slate had left it with its cleavage planes vertical, and into these the quarriers were accustomed to drive horizontal breast holes. Standing on flimsy-looking scaffolding on the high quarry face, with safety ropes draped around their bodies, they swung their hammers in wide free arcs. When they came to deal with other types of rock, no matter what the cleavage or bedding, they continued to use the breast-hole technique to which they were accustomed.

I must here diverge for a moment to mention that back at the Kentallen quarry the style of operation was again different. Here the stone was wanted in large blocks for dressing as ashlar. Deeper vertical holes were put down, and to each there might be three strikers, swinging their hammers round in full circle. Blasting powder was used to charge these holes, because of its slow action, and consequent less shattering effect on the rock.

For blasting in the ordinary cuttings gelignite was used. This had good shattering effect, which broke down the rock to convenient sizes for handling, and for ballast under the permanent way. But the gelignite was tricky stuff. In the winter if allowed to freeze it could be highly dangerous to handle, and so every rock ganger was provided with a kind of warming pan. This was a container surrounded by a hot-water jacket, and in it could be kept enough of the explosive in a thawed condition for immediate needs.

When the charge in each hole had been rammed home, a detonator attached to a safety fuse and set in a primer was inserted and the hole above filled with a tamping of sand or other suitable material. The fuse was a Bickford-type flexible cord with a core of gunpowder, and waterproof covered. The detonator was a small copper tube, closed at one end and half filled with fulminate of mercury. Into the open end the freshly cut end of the fuse was carefully inserted (for fulminate does not encourage liberties) and clamped in position. For the clamping a pair of pliers, suitably shaped, was provided for each gang, but it sometimes happened that a shot-firer, having left his pliers in the toolbox and not bothering to go and fetch them, bit the copper tight to the fuse with his teeth. I have never heard of a man accidentally biting on the fulminate and blowing his head off, but I should be surprised if it did not on rare occasions happen. The 'primer' was usually a half stick of gelignite about four inches long and an inch in diameter, with a hole poked in one end with a pencil-like bit of wood, and into this the detonator was inserted. The waterproof paper that encased the primer was then closed in above the detonator, tied to the fuse with a bit of string, and greased if necessary to keep out the wet. This assembly was pushed gently home on top of the main charge, the tamping completed as mentioned above, and all was ready for firing.

The men were cleared out, and one man went off in each direction to warn the public and all concerned by loud blares on a trumpet. It was characteristic of the gelignite that while it was liable to explode if set alight and the air excluded, it would burn freely in the open air. The usual practice of the ganger or shot-firer, therefore, was to cut a slice from a stick of gelignite, stick it on the end of his pocket-knife and light it with a match. It burned merrily and did not go out in the wind. He then scurried round setting a light to the various fuses and made his getaway in good time before the blasts started going off. The length of the fuses, of course, was cut to give him ample time to escape. The blasts were counted as they went off, and if there was any doubt, due perhaps to two going off together, a suitable time was allowed to elapse before a series of short toots sounded the all clear.

It was generally believed that gelignite was liable to be set off by impact, but Jimmy O'Neill, the ganger, who was full of strange notions and stranger stories, said he had tried to explode it in this way without success. He had hung a large stone from a rope carried through a fork in the branch of a tree, and tied the other end behind the tree trunk. A second large stone was placed on the ground exactly below the other, and on this he had carefully laid a stick of gelignite. Then hastily scuttling to safety behind the trunk, Jimmy released the rope and the stone made a bullseye on the gelignite. The zeal and enterprise displayed by Jimmy's enquiring mind deserved more positive results, but the explosive refused to explode. 'But wait you now,' said Jimmy, holding up a delaying hand. 'There was another time—it was at dinner time—an' I was just firin' the last few shots an' in a hurry to be away. When I clambered out of the cuttin' the bit of burnin' gelignite was still in me hand, and absentminded-like I poked it into me waistcoat pocket, the way ye would with a box of matches. It blew the waistcoat off me.' He was lucky that there could only have been a little bit of the burning stuff left or he might well have blown himself off the face of the earth.

Going down the road one day I met a sad little procession. One of the men had been charging a hole when the shot went off, and now his mates were carrying away what remained. It was a strict rule that only wooden stemmers should be used for pushing home the charge, because of the risk of steel or iron striking a spark from the rock. Here there had been no infringement, as the piece of wooden stemmer that protruded from the poor fellow's skull bore silent witness. Such accidents were not common, and their cause was obscure—a fragment of broken jumper that struck a spark from the rock? An extra jar that shook the sensitive detonator? The answer would never be known.

About halfway between Kentallen Station and Ballachulish Ferry the line ran through a long stretch of granite cutting. It could only be tackled effectively from the two ends, and progress was comparatively slow. Unless special steps were taken, there was likely to be delay in the general programme to get the cuttings through as quickly as possible, and so open up the route for locomotive traffic.

There came a day when a few of us assembled at this cutting to witness the trial of a new venture, drilling by machine. There stood the portable engine, housed in its shed of corrugated iron, well away from the cutting, its steam pressure well up. This would drive the air compressor standing nearby, and this in turn would drive the pneumatic drills. At first there had been a hitch, as something was wanted to complete the compressor. In the meantime an attempt was made to drive the drill direct by steam. It was said to have worked, but nobody liked it, least of all those who had to handle the hot pipes. Now all was in order and one of the percussion drills, mounted on its heavy tripod, was standing at the rock face. When the air was turned on it went like a bird, and in twenty minutes had drilled a three-foot hole in the hard rock. From then on there was a marked improvement in the rate of progress.

At first this innovation added something to the worries of the blacksmiths who had to sharpen the new drills. Some had been used only to the hand-drills with their plain chisel bits that could easily be sharpened on the anvil with a hand hammer. The new drills had cross bits that called for special sharpening tools and a change of method, but the new skill was soon acquired.

In scratching the surface of the earth for his utilitarian ends there is always the chance that the digger may uncover some fragment of history that had lain undisturbed for unknown years, recorded perhaps only in a name or a shadowy local tradition. Some half-mile south of Kentallen Bay there was above the road a small hillock, and in the green sward behind it was a slight depression a few inches deep that had always been known locally as the 'witch's grave'—no one knew why. It happened that the new line ran right through it, and there sure enough was unearthed a skull and other bones that might well have belonged to a small woman. The fact that the body had been buried in such an unusual spot would seem to lend colour to the implications of the traditional name. A box was made for the bones and placed on a shelf in the joiners' shop, pending some decision as to their disposal. Time passed and interest waned, until the eye of an acquisitive man in authority lighted on the box, and he was heard to remark that it 'would make a gran' box for haudin' dogs', these being the spikes by which flat-bottomed rails were fastened to the wooden sleepers. History does not record what happened after that, but I have a feeling that the bones of the unfortunate lady were reinterred in some unknown grave, un-coffined and without benefit of clergy.

9

The Wider World

EVENTS IN THE outside world kept marching on, and cast their pale reflection upon our smaller world among the hills. Soon after I joined the staff the Boer War had broken out, and some of our men went off to join the colours. One of the earliest was an assistant engineer, a quiet young fellow from the other end of the line who had been loaned for a time to the northern section. It seemed that there was hardly time for him to have reached the scene of the war when word came that he would not be coming back. Danny, the carter, an ebullient and hard-working egotist, wrote from the front to a pal to say he was getting on fine, apart from the restraining influence of the sergeant, who complained that he was much too brave. Soldier Grant, also a carter and formerly of the Gay Gordons, who still carried a very straight back, came in to his favourite dinner-time haunt in the smithy and complained sombrely of his hard luck. He had heard that ex-soldiers over forty were being considered for service again, and had written to his old headquarters. But the report was unfounded and they turned him down. Engrossed in the relation of his troubles, he forgot that the blue flame from a blacksmith's fire, fanned by the soft wind of the blacksmith's bellows, was not a thing to be careless about, until his tea, suddenly reaching the boiling point, sprang geyser-like into the air and left him with an empty drum and one more cause for lament.

Now and again a member of the local community would look in for a chat with the smith or anyone else whose duties brought him in with something to mend or sharpen (they were coming all the time), and who had to hang around till the job was finished. Across the road from the smithy lived old Mr. Downie the fisherman, and his wife. At times on a quiet day he could be seen fishing peacefully from his boat, anchored in the little bay. At this stage in his career I imagine he only fished for the pot, as I had never heard of him selling his catch. But at other times he would stroll across to the smithy to discuss the latest news from the front or put the world in order, a sort of honorary member of the club. A kindly man, round of body, comfortably filling his white moleskin trousers, and usually with a broad Scots bonnet on his head—about the only man I knew who still wore such a thing—his shrewd common sense, spiced with a pawky sense of humour, always gave a special savour to any discussion in which he became involved.

Near the Ballachulish Ferry one morning I heard the sound of martial music, and presently round the bend came a goodly company in full uniform, pipes and drums playing, and kilts and sporrans swinging—the Ballachulish Volunteers were on their way to the war. Of the reasons for this military movement the details are hearsay, and dimmed by time. But it appeared that a recruiting officer had visited the village a short time before, and been given an enthusiastic welcome. He may have been misled by this into expecting a larger number of volunteers than was justified, for when the solid results were assessed he sent a stinging rebuke by telegram. And now this was the reply of the village. I remember a remark made to me by the Quartermaster to the regiment: 'The Ballachulish Company is the smartest in the regiment. They march like one man.' Now here was the whole Company, marching with an added snap in their step, their spirits thoroughly roused by what they considered an unmerited rebuke, prepared to deal with Kruger, Staff Headquarters in Stirling Castle, or whoever got in their way. What happened in Stirling when it appeared that no quarters had been prepared for such an invasion is another story.

That summer of 1900, on a day in May, there came the news that Mafeking in South Africa, so long beseiged, and so gallantly defended by Baden-Powell and his little garrison, had at last been relieved. For seven months the people of Britain had eagerly followed the fortunes of the defenders, and now, like everyone else in the country who could do so, we clambered to the top of a hill and mafficked joyfully around a bonfire.

Life on the roads changed with the coming of the summer season. Ten times a day the busy paddle steamers came bustling in to Ballachulish pier on their run to and from Oban and Fort William, and discharged their flood of tourists, most of whom came from south of the border. Here four-in-hand and five-in-hand coaches awaited them to carry them swiftly along ten miles of narrow road to the Pass of Glencoe, allow them a short time to contemplate the beauties and glooms of that wild and empty glen, and then carry them back in time to board another steamer, for another step in their Highland pilgrimage. It might have been a scene from Dickens—the drivers and guards all gay in red coats and high hats, the grooms holding the heads of the fretting horses till coachman and passengers were all aboard, then stepping quickly back as each coach started and sped off down the road, the driver steadying the eager leaders from a canter to a swift trot, and the guard sounding a musical warning on his long horn as they neared the bends, while lesser traffic pulled in hastily to the side and gave them the road.

Could any finer way be found for travelling the open country than on the top of a coach behind a team of mettlesome horses? The red coats and the gay music of the horn; the racing blood of the horses echoing in the veins of the passengers; blue sky and sunlight and the moorland breeze; the whole orchestra of light and sound, colour and movement bringing sparkle to the eye and colour to the cheek. It is true that the sun did not always shine, but when it did, the memory of such a day would live while memory lasted.

Other more humble vehicles—brakes, wagonettes and traps— also met the steamers, to convey to the hotels those passengers who wished to make a stay. Porters from the two rival hotels wrestled for the bodies of such as had not already made bookings, and now seemed in imminent danger of being torn asunder, until one or other of the contestants had won the prize.

It was not only the wild beauty of the scenery that called people from far and near to view Glencoe. The grim tale of the massacre of the inhabitants in 1692 had spread abroad and shocked the hearts of men and women, both in the home country and in other lands. The story has long since passed into history, but it still stirs the imagination, and the scene of the tragedy draws many to visit the now empty stage. It may be well to recall here in brief outline the facts of history.

When in 1688 the last of the Stewart kings, James VII of Scotland and II of England, was driven from the throne, there were still many in the country who supported the banished monarch and refused to submit to his successor, William of Orange. Graham of Claverhouse, Marquis of Dundee, rose in rebellion, and on 27th July, 1669, he defeated King William's army at Killiecrankie in a swift battle. But he himself was killed and the impetus of the rebellion was lost. The Macdonalds of Glencoe had joined Dundee and fought at Killiecrankie. On their way homewards they were said to have raided the lands belonging to Campbell, the laird of Glenlyon, and carried away much of the stock, an act which can have done nothing to improve the relations between the two clans.

Two years after Killiecrankie the government offered pardon to all who had been under arms in the rebellion if they took an oath of allegiance before 1st January, 1692. MacIan, the chief of the Glencoe Macdonalds, delayed his submission till the last day of grace and presented himself at Fort William on 31st December. No one there had authority to accept his submission, and he was directed to Inveraray. He was an old man, a snowstorm delayed him, and it is not surprising that he did not reach Inveraray till 2nd January. Here he found that the Sheriff-depute was absent, and he did not return indeed till the 5th. The following day, after some hesitation, he administered the oath to MacIan. A certificate of this fact was sent to Edinburgh, together with names of others who had submitted. There, however, doubts were raised as to the propriety of placing before the Privy Council the name of one whose submission had not been received till after the pre-scribed date, and MacIan's name was accordingly deleted from the list. I do not propose to go into the question of who was to blame for the subsequent events. There appears to have been a good deal of intrigue in high places against the Macdonalds, and they had bitter enemies, including their hereditary foes the powerful Earls of Argyll and Bredalbane, both Campbells. There would seem to be still some doubt as to whether all the principal actors were aware of MacIan's belated submission, but whatever the facts of the case the upshot was that orders were issued by King William through his Secretary of State, the Master of Stair, that military action should be taken against those who had not submitted, and the Master himself confirmed that the Glencoe Macdonalds should be extirpated.

On 1st February a company of 120 men of Argyll's regiment, mostly Campbells, under Captain Campbell of Glenlyon, appeared in Glencoe and asked that they should be quartered in the glen, as the available barracks were overcrowded. (It was that same Campbell whose lands had been plundered by the Glencoe Macdonalds two years before, but here he was an officer of the army acting under orders, and it is not suggested that his actions were governed by any personal animosity.) The Macdonalds had no suspicions of any hostile intent, and for twelve days the troops were billeted up and down the glen and hospitably entertained.

Final orders were given to Glenlyon on 12th February that at 5 o'clock on the following morning he should fall upon the Macdonalds and put all to the sword under seventy. A stronger force of Argyll's regiment would be sent in support, to arrive at the hour of attack. And duly at that hour, before the breaking of a wintry dawn, the massacre was suddenly begun. Men were shot in their beds, or as they hastened out at the sound of the firing. Others were bound and shot in cold blood. The houses were burned to the ground by the soldiers, and the livestock driven away. The total number of Macdonalds living in the glen has been variously given. A figure of about 150 able-bodied men has been cited, and of these about a quarter were slain. Old men, women and children did not entirely escape the slaughter. A heavy snowstorm was raging and of the fugitives who got away to the hills it is probable that as many perished from cold and hunger as were slain by the troops; aged, infirm and children of both sexes, as well as able-bodied, driven to flight in such weather without food, or adequate clothing to protect them, what chance had they? In some ways, however, the storm did serve to help the fugitives; it aided the darkness to cover their escape, and it delayed by several hours the arrival of a body of troops who had been sent from Fort William to block the upper exits from the glen.

Many of those, both officers and men, who took part in this shameful tragedy must have done so with feelings of repugnance, and it is heartening to recall the tales that are told of individuals, obviously disliking the task imposed on them and seeking in devious ways to give to their hosts last-minute warnings of impending danger. This may to some extent account for the large number who escaped the actual slaughter.

It was not the cruelty of this massacre, savage as it was, that roused such bitter feeling and gave Glencoe its special place in the history of Scotland. Whatever our origin, who among us can claim that our forbears were guiltless of dark deeds of cruelty in the early days of clan and tribal rivalry? What stank in the nostrils of civilised men was the treachery—sitting at the host's table today and murdering him tomorrow, and so betraying the elementary rules of hospitality that even primitive man had learned to respect.

And now, two centuries after these events, as we slogged away at our railway building, thousands came by steamer and coach in the summer season in response to the compelling call of Glencoe. Perhaps, when we had finished our work and the trains were running, they would bring many thousands more to visit that lonely glen, full of its wild beauty and haunted by its tragic memories.

On a still day one could hear coming over the hills from twenty miles away in the direction of Mallaig the dull sound of explosions like echoes from the far-off battlefields. But it was only the blasting of rocks other than our own, to remind us that the line to Ballachulish was not the only one that was a-building, to make easier access to and from the heart of the Highlands.

On such a quiet day I was cycling along the road by the loch-side when I was arrested by a sound that made me dismount. The sea was smooth as glass, and from the Onich shore a mile away, clear but muted by distance, came across the water the sound of the pipes playing that heartbreak cry of sorrow 'The Flowers of the Forest'. Then I remembered. It was the funeral of one of those characters who from time to time come to enrich the quietness of the country scene with their store of wisdom and lore, and knowledge of nature and of their fellow men. His name was the Reverend Dr. Alexander Stewart, but he wrote a good deal under the pen-name of 'Nether Lochaber'. He wrote of birds and beasts, which he loved, and of the superstitions of country folk, and especially of all things Highland. From a friend who heard him speak at some clan gathering in Glasgow I heard a characteristic snatch of what he said, while his slow, sonorous voice penetrated to the far corners of St. Andrew's Hall:

'When I was a young man I could stand on Ben Nayvis and you would hear my voice over on Ben Cruachan! In my time I have met many of the great ones of the earth—Lords and Dukes and Earls—and if I wasn't a great man myself, I was a great Stewart.'

Now Ben Cruachan would hear no more the voice of the Great Stewart, and the pipes were lamenting him on his last journey. I have never heard the music of the pipes in a more moving setting.

IO

The Little Bridges

THE USE OF masonry, which had been for so long an important feature in railway building, and which has left its monuments in many fine bridges and viaducts throughout the country, was now dying out, and Portland cement concrete was taking the place of stone and brick in public works. The large bridges at Connel Ferry and Creagan are described in another chapter. For them stonework was used in the substructures, but elsewhere along the line the numerous smaller bridges, the station platform walls and other works of like nature were, with a few exceptions, to be of concrete.

The railway and the public road crossed and re-crossed each other at various points in order to provide the best alignment to accommodate them both.

Where the road was carried over the line the span of bridge gave the standard railway clearance of fifteen feet. Where it passed under the line the span for the roadway was twenty feet. There were also 'accommodation' bridges, usually with a ten- or twelve-foot roadway, for the use of the landholders, and still smaller 'cattlecreeps' of six-foot span to give access for cattle and sheep to either side of the line where severance of fields or grazing land had taken place.

Then there were the many streams that had to be crossed by bridges varying from ten to about forty feet in span, and innumerable culverts and drains of smaller size. The bridges generally, whether for road or stream, were with a few exceptions of arched type.

These minor bridge works presented few problems in their construction, but in putting in the foundations for the river bridges, in the loose, gravelly material that formed the bed of the stream, there was often some trouble in keeping out the water from the excavation. Whenever practicable, such work was done in the drier months of summer, when the streams were low. This, however, was not always easy, for these Highland streams are 'flashy', liable to rapid rise and flooding following a period of heavy rain, and a quick fall again when the rain has ceased for a few days. I well remember an occasion before the railway works were started when a wooden footbridge across the Duror River, leading to my home, was swept away in such a spate. The depth of the stream at low water was only a few inches, and the bridge was about eight feet above water level. During the night the three stout tree trunks that spanned the stream were carried nearly a mile downstream and deposited in the midst of a field. My father once told me that he had seen this same river come roaring down its channel after a plump or cloudburst, in a wall of water as high as a house.

Hand pumps and buckets were usually enough to deal with the inflow of water in the bridge foundations, and there was one primitive contrivance called a sludge pump that I only saw used on one job—the foundations of the bridge where the line crossed the Duror River. This pump took the form of a four-sided wooden box about six inches square and some ten feet long. The upper end was open and the lower end was closed by a flap-valve. The plunger rod was of wood, with a cross handle at the top and a leather bucket at the lower end. The contrivance rested slant-wise on the side of the excavation, the suction end in the sump and the other overhanging the stream. It was surprisingly efficient, but messy and awkward to use. Two, or possibly four, men could work it, pulling and pushing the long plunger up and down inside the box, but they had to keep clear of the cascade of water that poured out with every upward stroke. The thing was not popular.

Reference to this bridge reminds me of an occasion on which I was doing some work on the site while the excavation was going on. When the half-hour mid-day break for the men came round I nipped up to my home about a quarter of a mile away to get a bite. When I got back I found that Paddy, the ganger, had evidently been seized with a similar idea, or perhaps the sight of the sludge pump was getting him down. Anyhow, he had paid a rapid visit to the inn, a quarter of a mile away in the opposite direction, and was now back on the job in a rather incoherent condition. He tried to tell me something, but the words vanquished him, and finally he burst out with 'I musht have a shlape! I will have a shlape!' then stumbled across the Auchindarroch road and into the field beyond, where sleep overcame him and he collapsed and disappeared from view amidst the standing corn.

For most of the route the railway and the public road ran near each other, so there was little difficulty in delivering by cart or lorry the concrete materials required for such of these works as had to be constructed in advance of the track. There were also a few places along the line where materials could be delivered by sea. Kentallen Bay was one of these. The greatest bulk of material was concrete aggregate. This was either crushed granite from Lettermore or some other quarry, crusher-run from the specified maximum size to dust, or it was naturally graded beach gravel brought in by fishing smack, about twenty tons at a time.

At low tide during the night the smack would be loaded up by her crew of two at some not-too-distant part of the coast, then come in on the following high tide and beach near the site of the works, and at low tide the gravel would be unloaded into carts by our labourers and taken away to wherever it was to be used. The gravel was paid for at so much a ton, and where the smacksmen got it was their own concern, but in the case of one landowner at least there was outspoken plaint that his coastline was being illegally depleted.

When first this method of transport was used, a careful survey of the hold was made and the computed volume checked by measuring the first shipload in a 'banker' or bottomless box on the deck. Samples of the gravel were then taken and weighed, and very soon we were able, by inspection of the material and measuring the depth of its surface below deck level, to estimate very quickly the weight of the cargo.

Cement arrived by sea in two-hundredweight canvas sacks and

was immediately taken to dry storage. A shilling was allowed by the makers for each empty sack returned. This was worth salvaging, for a shilling was equal to nearly 2½ hours of a labourer's pay. The condition of the sack, however, did not seem to matter, so there was a strong temptation to take a few turns out of it for the handling of coal and other purposes before returning it to its rightful owners.

All concreting was done by hand. When the foundation of a bridge had been concreted the joiner came along and erected his shuttering, first a vertical row of battens nailed to a sole plate and then the planed tongued-and-grooved facing boards, brought up in stages as the concrete rose. Where, as was usually the case, the back of the wall would ultimately be covered by the earth embankment the shuttering on that side would be of a rougher character.

The concrete was mixed on a wooden staging, usually two twelve-foot-square sections placed side to side, and as close to the work as feasible. Half a dozen men filled the gauge box or banker with aggregate at the back end of the stage, and measured the cement. Then six men, working opposite each other in pairs, turned the batch over three times dry, turning towards the wall. On the third turn another man added the water, ideally from the rose of a watering can, but as this tended to slow up the work a bucket was more often used. Three more turns wet and the concrete was shovelled directly on to the wall if practicable, but if the layout prevented this, additional men wheeled it in barrows. A good concrete gang worked with the rhythmic precision of a machine.

On the wall itself at least one man saw that the concrete was properly placed and packed. Working along the face he would take up shovelful after shovelful and place it against the form, turning his shovel as he did so to bring it between the concrete and the form and agitating the plastic mixture to get rid of all the voids. He was often an oldish man of long experience and he would get an extra penny an hour for the job. He took a keen interest in his work, and seemed to enjoy it like a child puddling in the mud. Moreover, he was well aware that when the forms were stripped any 'honeycombing' or other blemish would be only too apparent to the critical eye. Old Tom Quinn was a good example of the type. Tom liked occasionally to leave his mate on the wall and go round the outside with a wooden mallet tapping on the forms, especially at awkward corners, to get rid of all voids and air bubbles, thus anticipating by many years the use of mechanical vibrators that would become in time a commonplace on any concrete job.

Just occasionally, when speed is of the utmost importance, Tom's job on the wall may be dispensed with. Perhaps there is much to be done yet to reach the required level and the shades of evening are fast approaching, or the tide is coming up.

'Come out o' that, Tom,' calls the ganger. 'See here, boys, stop chucking your stuff on to the wall. Throw it to hit the front shutter a foot up. Hit the boards every time.'

When the concrete is thrown to hit the forms in this way, just above the concrete already placed, the stones in the aggregate bounce back, and the fines remain against the forms and give a smooth finish. This saves any delay in waiting for Tom to finish his packing of the concrete, but it is indeed a precision job, especially with men at the end of a hard day, and only with a reliable squad would it be attempted.

In mass concrete of sufficient volume, such as bridge abutments and retaining walls, the use of blocks of good hard stone as 'plums' or 'displacers' was allowed. These were bedded in the soft concrete and kept apart, and back from the wall face, a distance equal to the width of a man's foot. The idea was to enable the man on the wall to pack the concrete thoroughly around the stones with his feet—a very effective method of consolidation.

The inspector blew the ganger up on one occasion for having the plums too close together, and challenged him to get his foot in between them. The ganger, a large man and also a man of some tact, explained that he had not assumed that a great hoof such as his own would be taken as a gauge, but rather a neater more normal foot such as the inspector's. Tension was eased, the inspector laughed, and as he had no wish to get his boots mucked up in the concrete, he contented himself with an admonition and moved on down the line.

It was astonishing to note how rapidly in the vicinity of concrete works the ground became cleared of all loose rocks lying around, and derelict dry-stone walls seemed to vanish overnight. Actually, the use of these plums was often a doubtful economy. They had to be collected and cleaned, and the placing of them in the wall tended to interrupt the rhythm of concreting. Nevertheless, many contractors liked them, and in the play of fun and games with the inspector their use had an irresistible attraction for the concrete ganger and his merry men.

II

Diverting the Roads

REFERENCE HAS BEEN made to the need for road and rail to cross each other at various places along the line. This meant bridging, and the construction of new road approaches to the bridges, whether the road passed over or under the line. Road traffic at that time being almost entirely horse-drawn, speeds on the highway were but a fraction of those allowed on the railway, and the road curves could, therefore, be designed to a smaller radius. This made the road alignment more flexible than that of the line, on which the smallest permitted radius was twelve chains, or 792 feet. In some places, where road and rail were crowded together along the narrow verge that separated mountain from sea, it was more economical to swing the road away from the line than to align the railway clear of the existing road.

Earthwork operations for these road diversions were on similar lines to those on the railway, but the formation of the roadway itself calls for special comment.

Over a hundred years before, towards the close of the eighteenth century, there was a strong movement on foot to improve the British roads throughout the country, which were at that time in a shocking condition. Prominent in that movement were two men of outstanding ability in the engineering world, John Louden Macadam, whose name is indelibly preserved in a type of roadway that is still in use today, and Thomas Telford, who, amidst a wide range of other activities, including the construction of 1,200 bridges, as well as canals, harbours and even churches, is reported to have supervised the building of a thousand miles of road.

But these two men differed profoundly on one question, the constitution of the road base. They were agreed in principle as to the wearing surface, and for this both men used stone broken to about 2-in. gauge. Telford, however, maintained that a foundation of larger stone, hand pitched, was necessary between the earth formation and the wearing surface coat. Macadam contended that no such foundation was required. His method was to spread the small-gauge stone uniformly over the roadway to a depth of up to ten inches and consolidate it thoroughly.

The engineers who determined the road-diversion details for the Ballachulish Railway evidently favoured Telford's system. The specification called for hand pitching nine inches deep. The stones were set on edge transversely to the road, with their broadest edge down. Any projecting points were knocked off with a hammer, and the interstices in the pitching filled in with small broken stone. On the top was a 3-in. wearing coat of 2-in. road metal. Consolidation of the surface was left to the traffic, which, both as to wheels and horses' hooves, was iron shod.

With the backing of such eminent protagonists as Macadam and Telford it may be taken that either of their methods, if properly carried out, could be depended upon to give a reasonably satisfactory road for the conditions then existing. Today the practice of pitching has largely disappeared, and few labourers now have the art of doing it. 'Hard core' of broken stone, brick or other hard material, consolidated with a heavy roller, has taken its place as a base course.

When railway and public road diversion ran close alongside each other a dry-stone rubble wall was often substituted for the usual railway wire fence. The stone was undressed as it came from the quarry, and the mason roughly shaped it where necessary with his hammer as he built. These walls were four feet high, one foot wide at the top, with faces slightly battered, and a spread foundation below ground level. They were topped with a cope about nine inches high of stones set on edge transversely, bedded and jointed in cement mortar.

The building of dry-stone walls is probably one of the oldest crafts known to man. At a very early stage our prehistoric ancestors who lived in caves must have got the idea of piling up stones at the cave mouth to keep out the storm or the prowling beast. Through the ages the craft developed with improving technique where suitable stone was available, and in more recent times the building of dry-stone walls for fencing came to be widely adopted in the hilly districts of Britain, separating field from field and strath from hill. Many of these old walls have no doubt been standing for centuries, a memorial to the skill of the builders. To build dry walls calls for greater skill, I think, than to build with the same stone in mortar. The mortar takes up any irregularities in the bed of the stone, and moreover a liberal application of mortar can conceal a multitude of faults. With dry-stone, on the other hand, it is stone to stone, with the quality of the work plainly showing, on the outside at least.

Building with rubble from a stratified rock is easier than from an amorphous rock like granite, for the stratified stone is laid on its natural bed. The result is also more pleasing to the eye. For the railway fence walls both types were used, taken from the nearest suitable cutting. The building was generally done by local men—a mason, who took the job on piecework, and a labourer—while Best provided all the materials and delivered them to the site. The difference in quality of the workmanship was very marked. Outstanding was that of an elderly mason, assisted by a lad in his teens—son or grandson. I fear it would be hard to find many of his kind today. As in so many other fields of activity, the product of the craftsman's skill is being replaced by something the machine can produce more cheaply, even if in many cases it lacks the quality of endurance that the older work possessed.

12

Off the Leash

AT THE DAWN of 1901 the great queen died, and an era came
to an end. The country was shocked and the world shaken, for
the long Victorian reign, which had lasted for sixty-three years,
had come to possess a quality of permanence that had drugged
the minds of men against facing the inevitable facts of change.

The Boer War would continue well into the following year,
but already the tide was turning. My two older brothers had gone
off, one a medical student and R.A.M.C. volunteer, to serve as
an orderly in the Scottish National Red Cross Hospital; his twin
a Lovat Scout. They both in due course came back. By the time
my turn came the war was drawing slowly towards its certain
end, and I decided to stay at home and get on with my bit of
railway building.

Thoughts of a holiday did, however, take hold of me. Glasgow
was staging an exhibition that year, a thing the city was rather
good at; they usually made a success of it. I had been to one
before, taken by my mother when I was a boy of six, and had
been greatly impressed. That, I think, had been my last holiday
away from home; it was time I had another. I arranged for a
week's leave.

When the archer unstrings his bow it is still a bow, and its
period of rest serves to renew its spring for further service.
When the soldier goes on furlough he is still a soldier, recharging
his mental and physical batteries for the next operation. The same
goes for workers in civil affairs, and I make no excuse for including
this chapter in the chronicles of the early days of the Ballachulish
railway.

About six o'clock on a summer morning I mounted my
bicycle and took the road that would ultimately lead me south,

a small kit tied on behind the saddle, and an oilskin strapped to the handlebars. It was good to be on the road, with the road to myself and not a care to bother me for the next week. Ballachulish was faintly astir when I passed through, but the road was almost empty. From Carnoch the Pap of Glencoe stood out bravely against the skyline. When I had swung past it and travelled a couple of miles on into the glen the emptiness was complete. Loch Triochaten lay peaceful and calm, reflecting on its surface the stern bulk of Aonach Dubh—the Black Ridge—that towered behind it, the near face dark and shadowy at this hour, and showing on its flank the darker speck of a slit that bore the name of Ossian's Cave.

As I pedalled along the winding road, heart high in the freshness of the morning, a constantly changing picture opened out before me of mountain and gorge that framed the narrow glen. Very soon the road began to rise, and I had perforce to dismount and push the bicycle up the steeper hills. This gave many opportunities to pause briefly and enjoy the backward view. I had rarely been this way before, and never beyond a well-known viewpoint called 'The Study'. Here it was the practice of the tourist coaches to make a brief halt and give their passengers an opportunity to look back on a view that for those who are road-bound and cannot scale the heights is, in its wild beauty, one of the finest in all the glen.

I would fain have lingered, but I must be pushing on, and pushing indeed it was. Two miles further on the road reached a point over a thousand feet above the sea level I had left behind, and after that the going was easier and the level fell a bit towards Kingshouse. The surface was of fine gravel, a kindlier stuff than the broken stone to which we were accustomed, and good going for a cycle, so long as one kept an eye open for the occasional larger pebble, up to first size, that could give the wheel a nasty jar, or even toss the rider over his handlebars.

As I passed the lonely hostelry of Kingshouse there was no human being in sight—perhaps it was still too early—but from somewhere around the premises appeared a deer, stepping daintily. From its air of possession it was probably a tame one.

It stopped and scrutinised me. Evidently disliking what it saw it chased me along the road, but having duly seen me off the premises it called off the hunt and went back.

The sun shone, the day was warming up, and the air was alive with scents from the open moor. Beyond Kingshouse the old road rose steadily up the side of the Black Mount for two miles till it reached its summit at about 1,450 feet. Away below to the left stretched the wastes of the Moor of Rannoch—bog and heather and broken lochans, their desolation chastened by distance and by the softness of the morning mists. Once over the divide I was glad to be able to coast for miles down the long slope on the other side, feet up on the rests in front clear of the whirling pedals. The free wheel had not yet come much into use, but those small brackets attached to the forks of the front wheel provided not only rests for the feet but a change of position as well. In later years I missed them. In that downhill rush there was something exhilarating in the foot-rest position that the free wheel seemed to lack.

Some miles on a female figure, cycling ahead, reminded me that the road was not mine alone. When a hundred yards behind her I saw a parcel drop from her saddle on to the road. I picked it up and took it on to where she had dismounted, and was rewarded with radiant laughing thanks from a bonny lass. Here, no doubt, was an opportunity to continue the journey in a more sociable setting, but with so many miles still lying ahead I told myself it was no time to dawdle. Or perhaps it was just that I was shy. I pushed on again.

Bridge of Orchy, Tyndrum, Crianlarich: I logged them all and noted the mileage. Crianlarich was where the two rival railways that served the Western Highlands met and crossed—at different levels—the West Highland above on its lordly viaduct heading for Fort William, and the Callander and Oban humbly at ground level on its way to Oban. The C & O was the parent of my little branch line to Ballachulish. How far away that seemed now.

Down Glen Falloch, and then the long twenty-mile run beside Loch Lomond, where the road was now busy enough by the standards of the day, especially around the little holiday centres,

Ardlui, Tarbet and Luss. Half an hour after leaving the lochside I reached the town of Dumbarton, where I had cousins, just in time for tea, and a welcome bath. My arithmetic told me that eighty-five or so miles lay behind me, but there was still some way to go, and with a certain reluctance I said goodbye. Offices seemed to be closing down for the day, and many people were hurrying homewards. Out in the road was another cyclist, one foot on the mounting step when I hailed him, asking the way to Glasgow. 'Follow me,' he called as he mounted. For fifteen miles he paced me into the city, and there with a wave of the hand he left me.

What I please to call synthetic relatives, that is those we choose for ourselves on our way through life, are often nearer to us than the kindred wished upon us by the normal processes of nature. My mother in her early days had a dear friend named Mary MacFarlane. In due course they were separated by time and circumstance and marriage, but ever remained like sisters. Mary married a gentleman named Stewart who was a measurer by profession, or what is known in other parts as a quantity surveyor, and practised in Glasgow. The ensuing families behaved like their mothers and were for all practical purposes synthetic cousins. The nearest to me in age of the Stewarts was Norman, a sturdy lad who ran with harriers in cross-country races, did things at the baths, played bowls and worked as a measurer in his father's office. The relations between the two families as I recall it was that when one party wished to visit the other they sent a note mentioning the date of arrival and size of contingent. Normally these visits took place in the summer, and if the city contingent was fairly large, or we had other visitors, we at our end simply overflowed into the barn or the long, low building that used to be the home of that other Stewart, James of the Glen.

I recall the occasion when we awaited the arrival of Norman, his older brother David (one of several), together with their parents. The lads left the train at Bridge-of-Orchy, and walked thirty-three miles by way of Glencoe, leaving their parents to continue the journey by train, steamer and road. Finding that the parents had not yet arrived they walked back up the road to meet them.

I may seem to be digressing from my narrative, but not so. I am merely giving a thumbnail sketch of the family that now welcomed me warmly to the city of Glasgow. A hearty meal was soon on the table, but even before that, Norman had me standing up on his bed while he gave my legs a brisk rub-down with flesh gloves.

We lost no time in the days that followed. Before breakfast I might be half a mile along the street looking at all the unusual sights that the city provided. My hostess chaffed me about this with gentle raillery. 'You'll see nothing at this time of the morning but all the wee skivvies cleaning their doorsteps!' But it was all fun to me.

Norman had his work to attend to, and during the daytime I often wandered about by myself, sometimes cycling, more often on foot. Looking back, it is curious to think that one could at that time, without undue risk, cycle through the centre of the great city, one hand on the handle bar, and the other holding a street map, threading a way through the horsedrawn traffic of carts, lorries, vans, cabs and trams, as well as other cyclists and the usual scatter of pedestrians invading the highway.

The town was full of visitors for the exhibition. Going down Sauchiehall Street I stopped a man to ask the way to the Mitchell Library. He was what I came to recognise later as a Glasgow type, not very tall, with a slightly rolling walk, slow and gentle of speech, dressed as befitted a responsible tradesman, his roots deep in the soil of his native city.

'Mitchell Library?' he said. 'Aye, Ah'll tell ye that. It's a pleasure tae me tae hear anybody askin' the way tae a library, when a' that the rest o' the folks is looking for is the exhibeetion. Come along an' Ah'll show ye.' In spite of protest he turned back on his tracks and walked along with me a couple of blocks to where he could point out the direction of the library without further risk of an ignorant stranger going astray.

In the evenings, when Norman was free, there were lots of things to be done. We went to the Albion Street Fire Station to see a turnout of the fire brigade, only a test alarm it is true, but the routine was the same as for the real thing. The engines, spick and shining, stood facing the door. From the ceiling hung the horses' harness, the collars open at the bottom so that they could drop straight on to the horses' necks and be quickly fastened, but there were no horses to be seen. There were no firemen. A shiny brass pole ran from the floor through a circular opening in the ceiling, which was closed by a trapdoor. Watches in hand, we waited. Then suddenly the alarm bell shrilled, and hard on the sound the trapdoor in the ceiling opened, and man after man fully dressed and helmeted slid down the brass rod. First man down pulled a rope hanging alongside, which opened folding doors at the back of the room. Here two horses were standing, and they hurried to their places in front of the engine, champing and fretting. Now a second was lost as one of the collars failed to clamp properly at the first slam. One man took the reins, one lit the boiler fire, which would come under forced draft as the engine raced to the conflagration. Swiftly all the crew were aboard and the fire-engine out in the yard ready to gallop off down the street. We compared watches: twenty seconds since the alarm went. 'Good enough!' we said, and went in search of further adventure. Outside in the streets the gas lamps shed a mellow light, and some of the shops were open. Once for a few moments we missed each other among the jostling walkers, but *rus in urbe* came to the rescue, and the call of a cock pheasant, heard above the noises of the street, and startling some of the passers-by, quickly restored contact.

We went one night to the baths, where Norman introduced me to the novelty of a Turkish bath, and also induced me to attempt—not very successfully—doing monkey-tricks with rings hanging over the swimming bath. I generally landed in the deep, as the easiest way out. Then there was the game of bowls. It must have been the Saturday afternoon when I had my first lesson. This was usually thought to be a game for the middle aged, but Norman had started early in his father's footsteps and played a good game.

There was, of course, the exhibition but, curiously enough, all I remember of this is that gala night at the fireworks. Along with a large number of other sightseers we stood and watched the display from some rising ground, where trees grew sparsely. We had a fine view, but after a time it occurred to me that an even finer view could be had from one of those trees, that no one else seemed to have spotted. A quick word with Norman, and I swarmed up the nearest. He followed, perhaps with an element of doubt in his mind, but he was always game for a ploy. Ensconced well up among the branches I found I was right. Here the view was indeed grand, and for a time I watched entranced the galaxies of bursting stars. I wondered why those people on the ground hadn't thought of this; perhaps being town-bred they weren't used to climbing trees. And then I became gradually conscious of other sounds than those of the fireworks—the murmur of many voices, punctuated by the sound of a persistent whistle. I glanced below to where my companion had been. He was gone, and on the ground I could see a large number of pale blobs that were evidently upturned faces, with a dark figure in the centre who seemed to be giving a solo performance on the whistle. Light began to dawn on me, and I swung down from branch to branch, to the running commentary of the crowd below, who seemed to be having the time of their lives. Such remarks as 'Yon chap knows the way he went up!' floated up from under.

I think Norman must have already been busy doing some tactful diplomatic work, for by the time I got down the policeman was off the boil, and contented himself with directing to me a few well-chosen words of admonition and advice.

The week passed all too quickly, and at the end of it I bade farewell to my good friends and set off in the early morning to return by the way I had come. The day was grey and heavy, and after the first thirty miles or so I began to get weary of the level monotony of the road. But when I had left Loch Lomond behind and began to get up among the lesser hills on the road, with their changing gradients, the weariness left me. Soon after Crianlarich, however, the rain began, and as the day wore on it increased to a steady downpour. For seven weary miles I pushed the bicycle up the inhospitable gradients of the Black Mount, and by the time I reached the divide I was past caring. I turned the bicycle upside down to tip accumulations of water, real or imaginary, out of the bearings, and mounted. Then with three parts of my journey behind me, and the worst of it at that, I put my feet up on the footrests and coasted gloriously down towards Glencoe, caring naught for wind or weather and dodging stray stones on the roadway as they came, my spirits soaring again.

13

The Appin Section

TOWARDS THE MIDDLE of autumn, when I had been two years on the line, word came that the engineer on the Appin section, a man called Shand, was leaving. I was asked if I would care to take on his job. I would indeed!

I had now to leave home, and found new quarters at Appin House with the manager of the home farm—they were old friends. For two years thereafter his good wife lodged me right royally as though I were the most precious of her numerous bairns. I moved in a few days before my predecessor left, so that he could hand over the work to me—paper work in the office, bench marks in the field and a hundred and one details. When he left I was at last on my own and the change was stimulating, though with plenty of things to worry a newcomer till he had found his feet. Mr. Wilson would come along every week or two to look over the works and see how things were going, and when there was any special job to do that called for two engineers or for more experience than I possessed, he would always come along to help me. At that stage in the construction, before the line was through, he would be driven by the coachman in the Boss's spanking pony trap, and sometimes the Boss himself paid us a visit. The distance, ten or twelve miles each way, was a long day's drive, and discouraged superfluous visits, but often they carried on to Connel by loco or other means, and returned another day.

Study was easier in lodgings than at home, for the evenings were now my own and generally free from interruptions. This was well, for in the study of books much evening, if not midnight oil, must be burned in the years ahead. From the window of my bed-sitting room there was a peaceful view of green fields and woodlands, with a glimpse of the loch and the hills beyond. A hard day outside was no disadvantage to study, for I found that, once established after supper in a comfortable chair, the wearier was the body the fresher became the mind for concentrating on books.

It will be gathered that there was scant provision in the district for the pursuit of knowledge by means of evening classes. But during that first winter at Appin Dr. Grant of Ballachulish, with commendable public spirit, gave a course of lectures on first aid in the Kentallen mission house: not specifically an engineering subject, but good for all men to know. I joined the class.

Kentallen was six miles from my lodgings. On the evening of the lecture (once a week or a fortnight) it was restful after supper to stretch out on two chairs for half an hour with eyes closed, and then, refreshed, to set off along the road. I do not remember if I ever bicycled when the state of the winter roads permitted: what sticks in the mind is footing it along the lonely miles in the darkness.

In the old days, when funerals went from Duror to the Appin churchyard, the coffin was often taken on a farm cart or carried by hand. Halfway along, with the nearest house a mile in either direction, the cortège used to stop for a rest, and it was the custom for the mourners to erect at the stopping place a small cairn of stones. It was always an eerie sort of place to pass, with the shadowy forms of the cairns half-seen in the night. When the first aid class was over for the evening I would go back the two miles to my home, and return the next morning to Appin.

The Appin section ran from Dalnatrat to Creagan Bridge and included the bridge itself, that is to say the foundations and substructure, which fell within our contract. My new quarters were ideally situated about the middle of the section, with the heaviest part of the work, including the bridge and the two railway stations, at Appin and Creagan, in the southern half.

The walking ganger had recently left, and in his place an energetic young chap had been promoted from ganger. His mother kept one of the workmen's huts, where he lived, but on his new appointment he had, in the interest of discipline, to leave the parental home and get into lodgings. The borderline between the responsibilities of the section engineer and the walking ganger was always a bit indefinite. They worked as a team, and I never knew of any disagreement, but from my point of view it was all to the good that the new man should be a fresher like myself.

My new office at Tynribbie was in a building shared with the stores and the saddler's shop. The saddler, a steady-going and contented-looking man in his late thirties, divided his time between the issue of stores, repairing harness and the making of a new set of gig harness for the Boss's pony that was a real craftsman's job. Later, when a telephone was installed, attention to this was included in his varied duties.

The erection of the permanent telephone line along the railway was being pushed on with all speed, and as soon as this was finished all the site offices throughout the works were connected, those of the resident engineer as well as those of the contractor. This was a great advantage. There was, however, but one party line, with a different calling signal for each office. It was, therefore, very unwise to indulge in the exchange of confidences, when any other office on the line might be listening in. The resident engineer related with glee on one occasion that after finishing a conversation he had paused for a moment before hanging up, and heard an awestruck voice that he recognised relaying the latest news: 'Three inches of snow at Ballachulish!'

In the field outside my office window horses grazed or lay in the sun, and nearby there was a stable infested by rats. Occasionally, when feeling the need of a brief change from my office desk I would pick up an iron-shod ranging-rod and betake me to the stable. Here a scurrying horde of rats would disappear like magic into their numerous holes, but if I waited quietly beside a hole for a minute or two a ring of beady eyes would appear, jostling for a better view of the intruder. When it appeared to me that the family circle was complete I went into violent action, but they were quick movers, and I do not recall that at the end of the engagement I retired with any substantial trophies of the chase.

There was also an office at Creagan Bridge, conveniently

placed by the roadside on the south shore, its windows over-looking the roadway, the narrows and the bridge works—an ideal site. Here one could work in peace, come fair come foul, with one eye on any special happenings on the bridge. Here also one made contact with some of the characters whose normal run was the Connel section, but whose general services included the bridge. There was the foreman carpenter, for instance, a sturdy and usually imperturbable sort of man who was responsible for staging, scaffolding and arch centring, including the driving of timber piles in the channel. He was called to the telephone one day and came back fuming. 'That was the Boss,' he said. 'He was complaining that derrick gantry isn't finished yet. Says he, "What have ye been doing since the New Year? I can smell your breath." Says I, "Well, ye've a damn fine scent" . . .'

Then there was the steam boss, Alick Woods, a brother-in-law of Alick Addison, and as unlike him as the proverbial chalk and cheese. He was tall and spare with a cropped moustache and a humorous and philosophic eye, a steady eye that had plenty of drive and ability behind it. His first contact with the firm of John Best was when he was employed by a firm of crane makers, and was sent by them to erect and test a derrick they had sold to the contractor. The performance of the derrick was tested against that of one provided by another firm. The test included picking up a load, luffing the jib, slewing round ninety degrees and lowering the load to the ground again. Alick had the whole performance finished before the other man got started slewing. He was promptly offered a job by the contractor and had been with the firm ever since.

From Woods I got snatches of information as to progress on the southern section. The old 'Jubilee' navvy was still digging away. 'It's a queer contraption,' says Alick. 'Nobody can drive it but the old-timer that came along with it, the time the firm bought it. They say he worked on the building of it, and he does most of the small odd repairs himself. But if anything big goes wrong and the fitters have to come in he just goes off and gets drunk, and he stays that way till the thing's mended, maybe for a week or more. Then as soon as it's fettled back he comes, and

so long as his pet machine is working he's as sober as a judge.'
'Look at him!' said Woods one day as we stood in my office, a
twinkle in his eye. I followed his gaze to the pier staging, where
Mr. Wilson, who had just arrived, was making one of his
energetic sweeps through the job. 'He whiles gets one of these
turns, goes dashing round the job, picking up an empty cement
bag somebody's left behind and chucking it somewhere else.'
Naturally I would not discuss my chief with a critical subordinate—even an old hand of the firm like Alick, but there was
no criticism in his voice, only a friendly admiration. Everybody
liked Wilson.

'You know Angus Weir,' he continued, referring to a man in
an authoritative position with whom we were both acquainted,
'Did you ever meet his brother James? No. Oh, yon man was a
hustler if you like. I mind one day he came on to the job and was
watching a cranedriver handling a tricky lift. He thought the man
was too canny about it, and after about two minutes up he jumps
into the cab, shoved the driver off and took the controls himself.
In about half a tick he had the whole contraption into the loch.
What a man! No, he wasn't drowned. You can't kill that sort.'

There was a canteen on the section, where hard liquor was sold,
and this gave us quite a bit of trouble on the works. It was placed
near the site of the new Appin Station, where a lot of work was
in hand, and it was found difficult to keep a sober ganger in
charge, with a pub a stone's throw away. Many of these men had
their fling at weekends, but no ganger could hold his job for long
if he could not reasonably be relied on to keep sober during the
working hours. One ganger who fell by the way complained
bitterly that the canteen was a trap to ensnare the men and make
double profits for their employer, and full of cursing and bitter-
ness he departed. He 'Gee-ho'd' the gang, but they did not follow
him. I tried, unavailing, to have the canteen closed. Long after,
when the line was opened and the offending canteen had in due
course been removed, the man came back, quiet and chastened,
looking for a job as foreman surfaceman, but regrettably we
could not then fit him in.

14

Boulder Clay

I HAVE PREVIOUSLY referred to the Dirty Cutting. Six hundred yards long and much of it twenty feet deep, it consisted of boulder clay under a covering of peat. Elsewhere throughout the line the slopes of 'soft' cuttings were taken off to a standard of 1½-to-1, which was considered to be the natural slope of earth, but here in the treacherous clay they were taken back to 2-to-1 to reduce the danger of slipping. In a spell of dry weather the clay was tough but tolerable, but its general condition was that of a gluey mass in which movement was difficult, and railway track slowly sank and had to be continually jacked up to level again. All-in-all it was a contractor's nightmare, each of its 40,000 cubic yards costing to excavate about double the price that was in the contract schedule.

The cutting was driven from both ends, but as it was on a 1-in-70 gradient falling towards the north, the south drive for drainage reasons could not be carried through at formation level. It was, therefore, first excavated to a rising gradient till the railway track was got through and then deepened to its final depth in a narrow cut. For this cut the clay had to be shovelled twice to reach the wagons above—a costly business. Then the track was lowered into the cut and the excavation taken out to its full width.

When first I saw it the Dirty Cutting was about half finished. The permanent way had been laid at each side to near the end of the cutting, with temporary track extended into the cutting itself. Pug engines ran the wagons along to the tip, most of the filling at that stage going towards the south, where there was a high embankment just beyond the site of Creagan Station. If the filling of the wagons with clay was a slow and laborious business,

The Dirty Cutting

The diver at Creagan

The author (centre) and his twin brothers

The navvy   The ganger

Work on a side cutting

Hand drilling

Creagan Bridge
Connel Ferry Bridge and the Falls of Lora

Connel Ferry Bridge under construction

Benderloch station in operation
MacBrayne's paddle steamer at Corpach

Next stop Appin: 30 October 1961
Crossing Creagan Bridge: 9 February 1962

Taking water at Creagan Station: a Sunday on November 1961

Summer excursion train departing Creagan Station: 30 June 1962

their emptying was swift and dramatic, and sometimes cata-strophic. Much the same procedure was gone through as with the horse-drawn wagons, but here the tipping was done by the loco, and the tempo was swifter. Moreover, the clay clung like a limpet to the wagons, and to minimise this the bottom of the wagons was liberally covered with sawdust before they were filled and the sides were sprinkled.

The driver of the loco was assisted by his fireman, more commonly called the roperunner, or 'ropey' for short, who also acted as shunter and jack-of-all-trades. A rake of four or five wagons would be taken down from the cutting and shunted into the siding near the bankend. One at a time they would then be taken out for tipping. On the front of the engine stood the ropey, one hand hanging on to the handrail, the other holding a long-handled hook threaded through a link of the coupling. The bankend man waved the driver on with short, jerky movements of his arm till the speed was to his satisfaction; then up went his hand, off came the coupling and on went the brakes of the loco. The bankend man swung his shovel into position to trip the catch, while his mate got ready to sprag a wheel a few yards short of the bumpsticks. The sprag was a piece of wood, usually of oak, about two feet long and four inches in diameter, tapered cigar-like at either end. It had to be thrust through in a split second between the spokes of a flying wheel, thus locking the wheel and making it and its neighbour on the same axle act as a brake. To do this called for a high degree of skill. There was also an element of danger in it, for if the man misjudged his movement the sprag might fly back and hit him. If all went well the wagon tipped. If something did occasionally go wrong and the wagon went rollicking down a thirty-foot bank, the only consolation was that a locomotive was a more powerful agent than a horse to haul it back again.

The clay itself when it reached the embankment was not content to stay there, but flowed slowly outwards like a greasy glacier and threatened to encroach on the public road that ran alongside. Along the toe we built a sturdy dry-stone retaining wall four feet high, but this was slowly pushed over in due course and we built it again. The clay in the meantime was drying out and settling, and after the second or third rebuilding the movement ceased and there was no more trouble—in my time anyhow.

There were cases in which the clay to be excavated was in a well-drained location, and here it could become very hard and tough, especially during a spell of hot dry weather. An example of this was the small subway leading to the island platform at Creagan Station. It was difficult to drive a pick into the clay, and explosives were used to break it down. Vertical holes were driven a couple of feet back from the working face by means of a bulb bar, that is a steel bar four to five feet long, swollen out to a pointed bulb at its lower end and driven down with a heavy sledge hammer. Light charges of gelignite were exploded in the holes, and gave good fragmentation to a size that could easily be shovelled.

Down the line at Tynribbie we had trouble of a different kind with this intractable stuff. Here a concrete arched bridge had been built to carry the public road over the line. It was noticed after a time that the bridge was slowly settling, as the clay supporting it gradually became compacted under the load, and the foot of the abutments had moved measurably closer under the pressure of the embankments behind. It was decided to arrest both movements by concreting an inverted arch under the line, to span between the two foundations.

A section of the line was taken up one morning, and a strong squad put on to excavate. By the late afternoon the excavation was finished and ready for the concrete. Incidentally, this excavating had removed some support from the two foundations, and their movement towards each other, while still small, had increased. Obviously the concreting could not be left till the morning, and that meant working late. The men worked well, but as the evening wore on and it got past their usual mealtime, they began to show signs of weariness. I called the nipper and told him to get his drum boiling for a cup of tea, and sent him to the nearby grocers to buy some bread and other oddments. (Early closing of shops had not then been invented.) The job was safely finished before darkness fell.

A week or two later I met the walking ganger. 'The men were looking for you last night,' he said.

'What men?'

'I kept some of the chaps on late to finish off a job. The first thing they said was: "Where's that man with the bread and jam?" You'll be spoiling them!'

15

Pug Locomotives

THE PUG LOCOS that served the contractor's purposes were hardy little tank engines, mostly four-wheeled, grubby as a street urchin by reason of their work, but often the pride of their crew, cared for and groomed like a beloved steed. At off moments of leisure you could see the driver wiping out his cab like a tidy housewife or decorating in banded patterns a copper steam pipe and watching while the heat painted the freshly polished surface in luminous shades of colour, whilst the engine hissed softly like a purring cat. Driver and fireman were a team: to be of any use they had to be, and to know instinctively each other's reactions, for swift joint action was often necessary.

The 1-in-70 gradient through the Dirty Cutting ran northwards for over half a mile. Any wagon that accidentally broke away from the cutting would, if left to itself, get up a high speed and go racing down the track and round the bends, a danger to anyone or anything on the line. To avoid this a set of catch points had been installed a little way north of the cutting. These were automatically set at danger, and any wagon getting away would be thrown clear of the track, doing itself no good but doing little damage to anything else. A man was in attendance to set the points to safety while traffic was going through.

On one occasion a wagon did get away during shunting operations in the cutting. It was spotted at once by Charlie on the footplate and Dod the ropey, who happened to be on the ground. Dod (short for George) was a bright lad, not long out of his teens, a young brother of the walking ganger; stocky and snub-nosed, as strong as a pony and as active as a cat.

'Let's after her, Charlie!' The loco was already moving as he clambered on board. Then a yell to the pointsman: 'Hold the points, let her through!' and Charlie's whistle shrieked a warning. The wagon, gathering speed, went charging through the catch points, but the loco was soon gaining, and before the end of the long straight was reached they were close behind. Dod the ropey, out at the front of the engine, tense, watched the closing gap till contact was imminent, then quickly slipped the coupling link over the hook, straightened up and waved to the driver that all was secure. Charlie slowed to a stop, and they towed the captured runaway back up the hill to the cutting, Dod grinning triumphantly as he wiped his brow with the sleeve of his coat.

One of the tasks for the loco that called for quite a bit of skill was turning a wagon to face the other way. There were side-tipping wagons for widening the embankments after the end-tippers had driven the road through. These side-tippers were bigger and heavier than the others and, therefore, more awkward to handle. From time to time one of them had to be turned around to tip on the opposite side. There was no turntable. In a slack spell or after normal working hours the wagon was run along to the nearest level-crossing of sufficient width, where the roadway was flush with the top of the rails. Here the ropey shoved a sprag into one wheel, scotched another and then carried a chain around the wagon in just the right position, one end hooked to the far end of the wagon and the other to the loco. A steady pull by the loco, and the wagon was slewed around off the track. A fresh hold for the chain, and in a matter of minutes the wagon was back on the rails and facing in the opposite direction. It looked easy when done by a competent team, but easier still for the inexperienced to end up with the wagon ditched and off the level-crossing.

These contractor's locomotives had to bear a lot of hard usage, and they needed to be tough to stand up to it. At one over-bridge on the Ballachulish section the approaches were both on a 1-in-10 gradient, and one of them had in addition a curvature of sixty-six-foot radius. Addison decided to do the filling with a loco and end-tipping wagons. The engine was not powerful enough to push a loaded wagon quietly up the curve, and it had to take it with a rush. The result was that every now and again the loco jumped the track and had to be laboriously jacked back on again, but Addison was not to be beaten, and he carried it through. Such treatment shook up the more sensitive parts of a loco, and emegency measures had sometimes to be taken. Leaking boiler tubes were a common trouble. If this appeared when the loco could not be conveniently laid off for repairs, one remedy was to give the boiler an injection of bran and water to act as a temporary stopgap. The bran was drawn towards the leaks and helped to seal them off. This practice had its dangers, as the tubes, partly protected by the bran from contact with the water, were liable to get burnt, but drivers in emergency would take the chance.

I was going down the line one day on Charlie's loco when trouble of this sort developed. There was no bran available, and at a place where road and railway ran alongside each other Charlie stopped the loco and sent his fireman along the road to look for some horse droppings that might serve as a substitute. Dod seemed to be having no luck, and when a horse and cart went plodding by he followed patiently in its wake with forlorn hope till the procession disappeared from our sight round a bend. But presently he reappeared in triumphant haste, his broad face beaming like the rising sun, and bearing in his tin a steaming fibrous mess. This he diluted into a thick gruel with water from the injector overflow pipe, and then while Charlie played with his valves to create a suction in the same pipe Dod offered the mixture to his pet with all the concentration and gentleness of a mother trying to tempt her sick child with a soothing delicacy.

16
___

What's in a Name?

I HAD HEARD of him first one day in the Ballachulish office.
Glancing at a printed report on the works canteen that was lying
on the table I noticed my name given as a member of the committee, and promptly demanded to know who had taken the
liberty of putting it there without my consent. I was calmed,
however, with the assurance that the reference was not to me at
all, but to a ganger on the Appin section who bore the same
name. When I took over that section he was still there and in
charge of the excavation of the Dirty Cutting. He was, I should
say, in his late thirties, about six feet tall, strongly built and
straight as a guardsman, and the wisp of silk kerchief that was
knotted round the muscles of his neck looked a trivial thing.
His men were Highlanders like himself, and he could do what he
liked with them. Normally he handled them quietly, but now
and again there were occasions when the volcanic forces inside
him seemed to surge to the surface, perhaps he was suffering from
a hangover—a rare event—or some hidden sore of the spirit, and
he would spray his gang with a running fire of commentary on
their shortcomings. I have a picture of him in my mind, standing
on the top of his cutting, his eyes half closed, while six or eight
of his patient men down below stumbled forward under the
weight of a 640-pound rail, their feet ensnared by the clinging
clay.

'What are you waiting for, you lubbers? Do you think you've
got the whole day to play around there? That's a metal for two
men: I'll take one end of her.'

The job of his gang was generally excavation, and sometimes
a bit of concreting, but in times of emergency some improvisation
has to be made. Going down the line one morning I found that a

platelaying squad had disappeared, leaving a length of track in pretty bad shape. The Dirty Cutting—the nearest source of man-power—was a few hundred yards away. I hasted thither and told Duncan to take his gang with their shovels and get the line put in order straight away. He would find the surfacing tools, screw-jacks, beaters, pinch bars and other oddments where the other squad had left them.

'I'm only a ganger, sir,' he said, 'I'm not a surfaceman.'

'You will be,' I said grimly, 'by the time I've finished with you.'

I spent an hour or so with him and then left him to get on with it. A grin was on his face when I came away: 'You should have been a platelayer, sir, instead of an engineer.' I have no doubt he meant it well, but it might have been better put.

Only once did we have something of a difference in the years I knew him, and the fault in a way was mine. The long summer days were with us, and the weather was perfect. Every effort was being made to get the line ready for opening in the early autumn, and some of the men were working late, while others were on the night shift. I had my supper and set off down the line again to see how things were going. The tide was well up, and at Dallens where sea and railway line were close together a puffer with a load of sleepers was at anchor off-shore. Men aboard, aided by the puffer's winch, threw the sleepers overboard into the sea. A small boat, moving about, edged them shorewards, and dominating the scene, thigh-deep in the water, stood Duncan with a boathook in his hand, thrusting at every sleeper within reach, while his voice ripped like a whiplash around the ears of his labouring gang.

I should have left him alone and passed quietly on my way. The sea and the air and the strenuous exercise would have done their work, and he was doing his job well enough. But I waited for him to wade ashore, and when he did I ventured on a quiet rebuke. That was all it wanted, the spark that touched off the explosion. He was off, he would go now. I tried to dissuade him, but it was useless. He wasn't truculent, as many a man would have been. He was remorseful but stubborn, and kept repeating that he wasn't going to stay on and be a disgrace to the clan.

'All right,' I said at last, 'I'm going down the line. Will you stop on and look after the men till I get back?' He agreed to that.

Further on I met Rory Matheson, who had been timekeeper on the Ballachulish section and was now our walking ganger.

'I hear Duncan's been celebrating,' he said. 'Were you speaking to him?'

I told him what had happened. 'I'm going back by the road. Perhaps by the morning he'll have changed his mind.'

'I doubt it. It's a pity you said anything to him. If you'd seen him as I have at Strome on a Saturday night, with four policemen trying to take him to the lockup . . .'

In the morning Duncan was gone, but within a matter of weeks he was back.

It must have been early the following year. The line had been opened for several months. I was standing on the island platform at Creagan Station waiting for the down-train from Benderloch, and at the other side the up-train was waiting patiently to proceed when the line was clear. Someone came over to me and said that Duncan's mother was in the train and would like to see me. His son, a laddie of about fifteen, had come down to see her off and took me across to his grandmother. A gentle old lady, dressed up in her Sunday best, she took my hand between her work-worn palms, while she spoke of her wayward lad, 'Poor Duncan', the tears running down her face. I did what I could to cheer her up with a few words in his praise that were genuine enough. And then the whistle blew, and I never saw her again.

17

Bridging the Narrows

FOR TWO-THIRDS of its length the route of the new railway was never out of sight of the sea. On the left the Firth of Lorne, succeeded by Loch Linnhe, thrust purposefully like a ragged spearhead towards the Great Glen. From this seaway three long fingers of salt water groped into the heart of the mountains, Loch Etive for eighteen miles, Loch Creran and Loch Leven each for about half that distance. Of these the first two had to be bridged to carry the line across. As for Loch Leven, many proposals had been made to bridge that also and link up with Fort William, but this was never done, and the new line swept round the southern shore of the loch to the terminus in the village of Ballachulish.

Of the two lochs that must be crossed, Loch Etive presented the greater difficulty in bridging. At Connel Ferry, near its entrance, the loch narrowed to a little over 200 yards in width at high tide. This was the obvious site for a bridge, but there were natural restrictions that governed the type of bridge to be adopted. The area of the loch is great, and its entrance forms a bottleneck, so that twice a day in each direction strong currents are created in the narrow channel by the rise and fall of the tide. At spring tides there is within a short distance a drop of three to four feet when the throttled flood goes raging through. It was this feature that gave the site the ancient name of the Falls of Lora.

All things are possible, but some are difficult. A design that called for the building of piers in such a channel was to be avoided and a cantilever type of bridge was adopted. The supporting piers of the two cantilevers could be sited in shallow water near shore, and the building of them carried out in open cofferdams. Moreover, the steelwork could be built out over the waterway without the use of supporting staging.

Between them the two cantilevers supported a central span of 232 feet. From centre to centre of the cantilever seats was a distance of 525 feet, giving a clear waterway of 500 feet, with 50 feet clear headroom above high water. Next to the Forth Bridge this was reputed to be the longest cantilever span in Europe.

A hundred feet or so landward of each cantilever seat heavy anchor piers tied down the back leg of the steelwork. Beyond the anchor piers the approaches were carried on a series of arches, three at the north end and four at the south, ending up with graceful curved wingwalls where the structure changed to an earth embankment. The piers and arched approaches were built of heavy granite ashlar. The substructure generally—foundations, piers and arched approaches—formed part of Best's contract. The steelwork was built by Arrol's Bridge and Roofing Company.

This has been described as a beautiful bridge. Some of those concerned in greater or less degree with the building of it were in two minds about that, but I think we all admired it for its strong functional simplicity. My own part in the work was small —an occasional visit of two or three days, either alone or with Mr. Rose, to help with some major setting-out operation. It made a welcome change of scene, and gave us a glimpse of what was happening at the south end of the line.

The Creagan Narrows, selected as the most suitable point for the crossing of Loch Creran, presented a different problem from that at Connel. Loch Creran extended little more than two miles beyond the bridge site, and, therefore, the volume of water that was forced by tidal movement to pass through the narrows was comparatively small. It is true that with a tidal rise of some twelve feet at springs the current at Creagan Bridge could be quite strong, but not to be compared with the tidal rip that went foaming through the Falls of Lora.

There was nothing here to discourage the building of piers in the channel, and presumably for this reason the design adopted was for a two-span bridge, with a central pier. Each span was 150 feet long, of steel girders, simply supported. Beyond each landward pier was an approach arch. The bridge piers and the approaches were to be of masonry—rock-faced granite ashlar that created no disharmony with the rugged hills around, and the whole was finished off in the romantic Scottish Baronial style, with crenellated parapets. As at Connel, the foundations and masonry fell within the contract of our firm, and Arrol's people did the steelwork.

At the north end the piers were founded on solid rock, above sea level. The centre pier and the main south pier were to be carried on steel cylinders, sunk by grabbing to a solid bearing. It was not expected that any special difficulties would be encountered, but to me much of the work was new and fascinating. If any snags did arise—well, so much to the good: was not the overcoming of snags the life of the engineer?

When I first arrived on the scene a staging carried on timber piles had been built in midstream, a derrick erected and the two cylinders that would support the centre pier were being pitched in position. These were suspended from the staging by steel rods in pairs, with long-threaded upper ends. When pitching was completed grabbing was started. The cylinders went slowly but steadily down under their loads of kentledge, which consisted mainly of short steel rails criss-crossed on the top. As sinking proceeded men with spanners slackened off the nuts on the suspension rods, and when the rods had reached their limit they were disconnected from the cylinder, one pair at a time, and reconnected at a higher level. These suspension rods not only controlled the movement and avoided the risk of any sudden downwards rush: they also kept the cylinders in position and prevented their getting out of plumb.

After some weeks movement of the first cylinder stopped, and the addition of more kentledge would not budge it. A diver went down and reported that the cutting edge at one side was sitting on a steeply-sloping surface of rock. Consultations took place at a high level, and it was then decided that the rock must be levelled off, and that compressed air should be installed to enable this to be done in the dry. An inner cylinder was accordingly fitted, and a small air lock erected at the top. The possibility of this having to be done had been foreseen, and the base ring that formed the cutting edge had been designed for the easy attachment of an inner cylinder that would act as an air shaft.

An experienced compressed-air worker was sent from headquarters in Edinburgh to get work on the cylinders going. When I first met him on the site the compressor was chugging away quietly, and the water had been blown down inside the cylinder. He had already been down to have a look at the job and seemed discontented with what he saw and with things in general. Most of his conversation was concerned with the things that had not been provided for him, of which I can only recall dry socks.

'Will you come down, engineer?' he asked at length.

I knew next to nothing about compressed air, and was rather scared of the thing, but I couldn't tell him that.

We crawled into the air lock, and after the appropriate time for the pressure to build up, he opened the interconnecting door and we clambered down the ladder inside. The water had been lowered as far as the cutting edge. Below that level the air escaped through the gravel, and as the grab had dug a hole down the sloping face of the rock there was a foot of water in the bottom, which was evidently one of the causes of complaint.

The only result of decompression on the way out was a drop or two of blood from my nose, and this recurred whenever I went down, and did me no harm. Air pressures were not high, not, if I remember aright, much above double atmospheric pressure, and did not reach the danger limit. We had no cases of 'bends' or caisson disease, a condition due to concentrations of nitrogen in different parts of the body, when men have been working in high pressures and have been too quickly decompressed.

I do not think the man stayed long with us, but we lost no time in training some of our own men to work in compressed air. The first volunteer was an able-bodied stonemason, but he had a tendency to nasal catarrh, and at his first attempt in the lock he had to give up, as the rising pressure hurt him. Other men, however, took to the work with no trouble, and the operation of levelling the hard rock went steadily on, using plug-and-feather, wedges and chisels. The debris was hauled up by hand in a bucket, attached to a rope that ran through a pulley in the ceiling of the air lock.

When the two cylinders were successively grounded on a solid bearing they were quickly filled to the top with concrete by means of a tremie. This is a long pipe or box let down into the water till its lower end reaches the bottom and the top is still above water. It is filled with concrete while it is being lowered, and if the depth is considerable it may be necessary to add one section after another as it goes down. The outlet at the bottom has to be temporarily closed by a trapdoor or plug to prevent the concrete running through till the tremie is grounded. Then the concrete is allowed to flow steadily through the tremie, which is slowly raised as the level of the concrete rises, but the foot of the tremie must always be kept well buried in the fresh concrete, otherwise its contents are discharged with a rush that disturbs the water, washing apart the cement and aggregate. This can result in very bad concrete, which may in some positions never afterwards be detected, unless its weakness becomes the cause of a failure. For this reason underwater concreting must always be carried out under experienced and trustworthy supervision, and just because of its peculiar difficulties it will always be a fascinating operation.

The compressed-air work took us about three months to complete, and then the faithful little compressor, which had run non-stop all the time, was dismantled and taken away.

At the south end of the bridge it was possible to continue the sinking of the cylinders in the open until they reached their final level, but the progress was slow. The ground was composed of gravel and small boulders, and the boulders were liable to get wedged under the cutting edge. A diver had, therefore, to keep going down and digging them out with pick or pinch bar and dumping them in the centre, where the grab could easily reach them. The divers seemed to dislike working in these confined spaces; it might be an innate fear that if the cylinder went down with a jerk (as sometimes happened) some of the kentledge might be dislodged and drop on them. Perhaps this was why, when I suggested that I might go down myself and take a spell, there was no objection at all, although divers are sometimes touchy chaps. But Alick Woods, who was in charge of the operation, insisted in bringing out a clean diving dress: one of the divers, he said, had a nasty habit of spitting in the bib.

When these cylinders were duly sunk and concreted they were connected by a heavy mass-concrete cap, constructed inside a cofferdam. The first layer of concrete was placed under water, taken up to a level that would bring it above low tide. When the tide went out the surface of the concrete was covered by a grey, slimy layer over two inches thick. This was my first experience of laitance in any quantity, a deadly enemy of underwater concrete. It is mainly washed out from the cement, and by itself it will not set. Here it was harmless, as it could be cleaned off, but in deep-water work it is liable to form in large pockets, and careful steps have to be taken to prevent this happening, or clear out the pockets before the next layer is placed above. It is, of course, inevitable that some cement is lost in underwater concreting, and to allow for this it is usual for such work to provide extra cement in the mixture.

The distance across the narrows had, of course, been accurately measured in the early stages, probably by triangulation, before the work was begun. Now the two spans were checked again by means of a fine steel piano wire stretched across the channels, and the exact positions of the landward piers established.

As foundations were finished the masons moved in, and soon the piers were climbing slowly but steadily skywards. The foreman mason, whose name was Drummond, was an old hand of wide experience, and had a family of mason sons following in his steps. Whether moving about from one part of the work to another and giving orders, or standing in a prominent position where he could overlook a large area of activity, he often clutched in one hand a crumpled cloth tracing as though it were a duster, and this he would consult from time to time to check some detail of the building.

On the slender centre pier the chief problem was lack of space. There was little room on the top for storing materials—the squared granite facing blocks, the rubble for hearting and the mortar, as well as for the masons themselves who built all these things into an enduring structure. Hence the derrick that straddled the deck of the adjoining staging had to be in constant attendance to hoist up the materials load by load as the builders required them. One of the foreman's sons deputised for him on this pier, for, active as he was, the regular scaling of long ladders was hardly consistent with his advancing years.

The cramped working space on the top of the pier got young Drummond into trouble on one occasion. A Mr. Crutwell, a consulting engineer who was associated with Wolfe Barry in the design of the Connel and Creagan bridges, paid a rare visit to the site. I found him climbing down from the top in a state of great annoyance. He complained that the hearting of the pier was being built dry, without any mortar, and if it was all like that the pier would certainly fall down. I clambered up the ladder with him again, and learned what had happened. Normally the derrick was in constant attendance, and hoisted up the stone in small quantities as required by the builders. But on this occasion it appeared that for some reason, probably for minor repairs, the derrick had to be taken off duty for a time. To ensure that he had plenty of stone to keep his masons going in the interval, the foreman had got an ample supply hoisted up and dumped in a heap on the top. From this he would take the stones as required, levering out the heavier ones by hand, and bed them solidly in position. But his zeal had been excessive; the pier was over-crowded, and at first sight there was some reason for the eminent engineer to fear that the work was being badly scamped. I did my best to reassure him, and the timely and unexpected arrival of Mr. Wilson saved me from annihilation. He diverted the blast of the storm to young Drummond, and succeeded in restoring a measure of calm.

At the shore ends, as soon as the level of the arch springing was reached, the wooden centring was erected by the carpenters and supported on 'folding' wedges, that is to say, on pairs of wooden wedges laid horizontally one above the other and facing in opposite directions. These could be easily knocked out later when the time came to strike the centring. As the granite voussoirs were laid, arching between the piers, the arches completed, and the spandrel walls rising above them, then the approaches really began to take on a satisfying appearance of unity and purpose. A rowing boat was in constant attendance at the bridge during working hours, not only to ferry passengers to the centre pier or the opposite shore, but also as a standby in case anyone fell into the sea or any timber or other floatage got adrift.

'Who is that Englishman?' asked a visitor one day as the voice of the ferryman, talking to a distant colleague, came clearly up from the boat.

'His name's MacKenzie,' I said. 'Wait till you hear him talking Gaelic.'

He was said to have been for many years in household service in the south of England, and was commonly referred to as 'the Butler'. In the course of the years his accent had changed, not to a hybrid 'Englified' style so common in such cases, nor had he copied the accents of the servants' hall. Consciously or otherwise he had acquired the cultured English of his employers and their class, and in both language and appearance he would have passed for a rather superior type of English peer. His brother, on the contrary, who had a small farm in the district, spoke with a fine old homespun accent that was as Highland as a peat.

When the centre pier and the arched approaches had reached their final height, and before the parapets were built, the steel people came on to the scene. They put up two temporary piled trestles in each of the channels, and started erection of the steel-work, and soon the hills were echoing to a new sound—the rattle of the riveting hammers. Working as they were out over the open channel, there were happily few accidents. On one occasion a rivet boy missed his footing and dropped with a resounding splash into the sea fifty feet below. When we heard him yelling we were comforted by the knowledge the noise conveyed that he wasn't either dead or too badly hurt, and the boatman was speedily on the spot and hauled the lad on board. I found the steel foreman energetically applying first aid by the novel process of twisting his arm to make him sick and so get rid of any of the waters of Loch Creran that he had inadvertently swallowed. The treatment, however, appeared to be unnecessary. The boy had hit the water first with his head and right shoulder, and both the shoulder and that side of his face were swollen and black and blue, and one eye was bunged up. There were no signs, however, of serious injury.

The structure of the steelwork crept slowly forward as member after member was slung into position and bolted, prior to its final riveting. I found one morning that the erectors had thrown a twelve- or fourteen-inch baulk of timber across a ten-yard closing gap in the north span. I wanted to get to the centre pier and the short cut looked tempting. It would save me going down to the ferry and climbing again up the pier. To a steel erector walking the timber would have been as easy as walking on the ground. Normally heights never bothered me so long as there was something to hang on to, and if there had even been a bit of flimsy tape strung along the side at handrail level to give the semblance of support it would have made all the difference. Before I was halfway across I seemed to have grown to about seven feet high and top heavy, and the tide racing through away below did nothing to help. However, by a strong effort of imagination I managed to get my centre of gravity down to about ankle level and to keep it there, and so was able to carry on without the need to get down ignominiously and finish the course on all fours. I mention this as an interesting example of the part played by the imagination in questions of height and balance.

Some years afterwards the head of a firm of steelwork contractors remarked on this, as from my office window we watched one of his erectors, silhouetted high up against a windy sky, walking along a six-inch channel.

'He's incredible, that chap,' he said, 'quite out of the ordinary. The foreman tells me he's a Finn. But it's surprising, when we come to build in a new part of the country, how little difficulty we have in adapting the local labour to erection work. Not all of them, of course: some can never take it. But ordinary men who have never done anything like it before start at ground level and go up with the building, and so get used to heights without noticing it.'

For one reason or another there had been some delay in the progress of the two bridges, particularly the Connel Ferry one, and fears were expressed that these important works might not be finished to schedule, and so might delay the opening of the line. About this time I met an engineer in his early thirties named Cecil Booth, who had been sent by Arrols to speed up the steel-work erection. He had behind him a good record for his work in connection with the erection of the Big Wheel at Blackpool, and having looked into the matter of the bridges he was reported to have said quite simply that he would finish to schedule if he had to put a man on every rivet. Later he was to become better known, though not perhaps as well as he should have been, as the inventor of the vacuum cleaner.

18

Laying the Rails

WE WERE NOW beginning to get into the last stages of the work. There was still much to be done, but as cutting after cutting had been opened through and the embankments finished, the gaps in the permanent way had been closed, and now the twin ribbons of steel gave a coherence to what had earlier seemed like a number of separate operations. But first in each gap there had been a checking over of the level of the formation, then the bottom ballast of broken stone was laid, nine inches deep, and where practicable the permanent rails were strung along the side before the temporary track was taken up.

The 80-lb. bull-headed rails, 32 feet long, with their chairs and fittings, were provided by the railway company, and would have to be accounted for when the contract was finished. There were also second-hand rails of the same type, 24 feet long, loaned to the contractor for use in his temporary works and finally laid in the station sidings.

The sleepers were of pine or spruce, creosoted, but at one place on the Appin section the contractor took over a small forest of larch and installed a sawmill to cut up the logs for sleepers. This timber was very dense and resinous, and creosoting of the larch sleepers was considered unnecessary.

The actual laying was often done by piecework. Being a repetitive job, it gave plenty of scope for ingenious planning of the different operations, and a well-organised gang could get rewarding results. Sleepers and fittings were brought forward to the railhead by the loco and handed over to the gang. Men in pairs took the sleepers for the first length of rail and strung them out roughly in position, twelve to the 32-foot length. The rails were then lifted by hand into position, keyed to chairs at middles and ends, and fishplated to the last laid pair, leaving an expansion gap of $\frac{1}{8}$ to $\frac{1}{4}$ inch at each joint, depending on the time of year and temperature. A hand bogey could now be pushed along carrying the chairs, keys and fittings, and the sleepers for the next length. Meanwhile a man measured along one of the rails just laid, and marked in chalk the position of each chair, then, using a square, he marked the position on the other rail. Other men followed him, fastening the chairs to the rails with wooden keys, positioning the sleepers and spiking the chairs to them. A gauge was in constant use for the final spiking, for although the sleepers had already been accurately drilled for the spikes, it was possible in driving to get slightly out of position unless the gauge was held.

As the work advanced the track was roughly but solidly packed to allow the loco and its trucks to follow closely and so minimise the amount of hand-carrying. Later another surfacing gang would follow, adjusting the track to its proper line and level, and raising the outer rail on curves to its specified cant. Each sleeper must be packed tight underneath from its outer end to nine inches inside the rail, but the centre only loosely shovel-packed, for if this bit were bedded too hard the sleeper would be liable to break its back under load of the train. Then the top ballast of gravel or of stone broken to a smaller size than the bottom ballast was filled in to sleeper level, both between the sleepers and outside their ends.

This final adjustment of the line may give the section engineer quite a bit of work. He has the centre line of the track to set out all over again—straights and curves and the transition curves that are put in between them to ease the change when the radius is very sharp. Many of his fixed points have got lost or damaged by blasting. The rail levels will also want checking, and the bench marks may also have got lost or become unreliable, in which case he must check back to the nearest reliable Ordnance Bench Mark. He has to see that the ganger has the right cant for every curve. The cant varies with the radius, and where the curve is exceptionally sharp a check rail may also have to be laid. Going down the line he may be accosted by the ganger of the surfacing squad with a request like this:

'Would ye mind gettin' out yer theoddley one o' them days and givin' me a few points down the straight?'

'Theodolite! What do you want that for on the straight? Surely you can line that up yourself.'

The ganger gives him a quizzical look, and wags a horny forefinger in disagreement.

'Any old navvy,' he says, 'can eye in a curve, but it takes an engineer to set out a straight line!'

There is always satisfaction in the final clearing up that takes place when a job is nearing its completion. For years, perhaps, the works and often the roads adjoining them have looked like a battlefield (one cannot make an omelet without breaking a few eggs), and now it is possible to introduce some suggestion of tidiness and regard for future amenity. The old railway companies were particular about the appearance of their lines, and paid the contractor to soil and sow with grass seed all slopes of earth cuttings and embankments, and thus as far as possible avoid unsightly scars. Hence, in country where rough moorland and sparse-covered rock were rife, arose the need to strip and conserve any suitable soil when opening out a cutting, as mentioned in an earlier chapter, and hence also the reason why these new works mellowed so quickly and merged happily into the surrounding landscape.

I have no record of the total number of men employed on the contract, but from recollection I would place it at about two hundred on each of the three sections when going full swing in the summer, and fewer in the winter months. The scarcity of labour was always a problem, and in the last year of construction, with the date for completion looming up in sight, this problem became more acute. Processions of unemployed paraded the streets of Glasgow, but they seemed to have no urge to leave the bright city lights and go where work was to be found. Arrangements were made to bring a batch of them through by rail, but few if any stayed. In the warm summer sunshine a scatter of drunks could be seen lying prone around the nearest pub like spilt matches, but when any money they had was spent, the reports were that they stole anything they could around the countryside and tramped back to Glasgow. There was, however, one source of labour that gave us unexpected help towards the end of the contract. The Ballachulish quarries went on strike. The reasons for this novel departure in industrial relations in the Highlands need not be gone into here, but many of the men came to us for work. When the permanent way had been laid through from Ballachulish to the Appin section, a train of wagons brought the Ballachulish men in the morning and took them home at night. A night shift was put on to certain jobs, and the same trains served for their transport in the opposite direction. A sense of urgency pervaded the whole line, and the good weather was helpful. The Dirty Cutting was one of the last of the major obstacles to be overcome on the Appin section. From a couple of faded snapshots I have recently unearthed, it would seem that four months before the line was due for opening a great deal of clay had still to be laboriously dug out. But at length it was bottomed, and then, before the permanent way was laid through, an extra depth of two feet of clay was dug out below the formation, and refilled with good material, to give a better bearing to the ballast that carried the track.

Work on the laying of the station sidings went ahead now, using the old worn rails that had already done good service in the company's main line somewhere else, as well as in the contractor's temporary tracks during construction.

19

Building the Stations

WHEN THE TIME came to get on with the station building, it was suggested that the platform walls might be built of stone. Creagan Station had an island platform, the up line curved and the down line straight. A start was made with the curved wall. When this had been built about two-thirds of its height it was not a very creditable-looking job. The stone was hard, with erratic cleavage, and not too easy to build with, and it might perhaps be that the mason was not used to that class of work. When Mr. John Ferguson, the consulting engineer, came round a few days later on one of his periodic visits he complained crisply to Mr. Wilson that the wall was neither to line nor level nor anything else. The section engineer, of course, was responsible and took the backlash of that. The upshot was that it was decided to complete the remaining overhanging portion of the wall in concrete, and to use concrete only for the other wall. Mr. Ferguson, though outspoken in criticism, was always fair, and ready to give credit where it was due. When next he visited the site the straight wall was well ahead, and he came out of his way to remark that my joiner, who erected the wooden forms, had a very good eye.

It was shortly after this that I first met old Mr. Richards, the inspector from the southern section. He was about seventy years of age, a mason by trade, and very knowledgeable. He was also the father of Inspector Ben Richards of the Ballachulish section. He was seated in the little site office at Creagan Station when I was introduced to him, and I took to him at once. He apologised with simple dignity for not getting up to greet me: 'I've got a boil on me backside,' he explained.

He had been sent by his chief to rebuke us for using pinnings in the face of a dry stone retaining wall. But old Richards knew his job, and was no 'yes' man. He took a brief look at the wall and delivered his verdict: 'Of course you need pinnings in the joints of a dry-stone wall; you can't make a proper job without them.' Like Balaam of old, he had been sent to curse and instead had blessed.

We talked of various things, and in the course of a discussion about concrete he made a remark that arrested me: 'They say that the less water you can use in mixing your concrete, the stronger it will be.' This was a new idea to me and I thought it over. We had no means of making tests on the site, but I decided to try out the idea. George the joiner was by this time putting up the forms for the broad overhanging granolithic coping that topped the platform walls. He was a good man and very keen on making a good job, and he had asked if I would allow him and his mate to concrete the cope as well as put up the forms, and so avoid having a concrete gang messing about with his work. ('Lines of demarcation' had not yet been thought of on public works.) I had agreed to this, and George had made a start on the concreting. The cope was laid in alternate panels eight feet long, so as to avoid unsightly cracks as the concrete shrank. Here was the opportunity to try out the new principle. George fell in with my wishes, but after a time he found my zeal a bit irksome, and he showed signs of rebellion, for dryish concrete is more difficult to work into a compact mass than is wet concrete. Indeed at one point there seemed a risk that I might lose a first-class joiner, but we managed to come to a compromise.

As we are on the subject of wet concrete, perhaps I may break off the narrative for a moment and look forward some twenty years to the occasion when first I had an opportunity of testing properly the view quoted by old Mr. Richards as to the effect the proportion of water used had on the strength of the concrete. A certain Professor Duff Abrams in the U.S.A. had been propounding a law, or a theory, that the strength of concrete depended on the ratio of water to cement, regardless of the amount of aggregate used, so long as the mixture was workable —not too wet, not too dry. I was on a large job in Northern

Quebec when I first came across this man's writings. At the first opportunity I rounded up one of the university graduates who had replaced the old-fashioned type of inspector in the supervision of the concrete—a keen lad who was as interested as I to test the theory. In the laboratory we measured and mixed up a sloppy grout of cement and water, filled a test mould with some of this and set it aside. Then we added some aggregate and filled another mould and continued adding aggregate and making specimens till the mixture became unworkable. After a suitable number of days, when the blocks had set hard, we crushed them in the testing machine. With the exception of two ends of the series, the one too fluid and the other too dry to compact, all the blocks had much the same strength, thus satisfying us of the soundness of the water–cement ratio law. This is a most interesting principle, which since then has been accepted and used in practice all over the world. But here we must be careful, and not assume that we have found the answer to every problem of strength design. For cement and aggregates vary in strength. Some aggregates are also harsher than others and require more water to make them workable, and more cement to compensate. As workability is not a matter of theory or formula, but of practical experience, we are back where we were in the hands of the practical man.

I was back in the vicinity of Creagan Station some fifty years after the line was opened, and took the opportunity of inspecting again the concrete coping of the platform walls that George had laid so carefully. The line of it had become just a trifle wavy, for the clay foundation, hard enough as it had seemed when we founded on it, is always sensitive to changes in its own humidity. But it was gratifying to see how the concrete had stood up to fifty years of the tread of tackety boots. And then I noticed that the alternate panels, while still sound, showed slightly more wear than their neighbours. That set me thinking, and I wondered whether, after I had visited him each day and passed on down the line, the good George had taken it upon himself to interpret my instructions with just a little fluidity.

I have been asked in recent years how I thought that modern concrete compared with that of the earlier days, and I should like to make here a few comments on that. In the twentieth century, particularly since the First World War, we have greatly advanced in our knowledge of cement, in our methods of design and in our making and placing of concrete. Cements have been devised for different conditions and for different purposes, too numerous to mention here. The designer has moved from mass to reinforced concrete, which a few years ago was in its infancy, and which now, with its latest refinements, has revolutionised the whole outlook on structural design. With regard to the making of the concrete, the greatest change is mechanisation—the concrete mixer, the concrete placer and, not least, the mechanical vibrator, which is a great advance on old Tom Quinn's wooden mallet, and without which it would be very difficult to attain the high strength required for the most modern types of structures.

But not only is the machine capable of great good, it has also power to do much harm. The motor car mishandled on the road can do more damage than could the runaway horse. The concrete mixer can turn out a batch of over-watered slurry that the labourer's shovel could not handle. The misused placing machine can do more harm to the wet concrete by segregation than could the more primitive methods of handling.

It is not to be thought that the old navvy ganger and his squad always produced perfect concrete; far from it. They were only too prone, when the inspector's eye was not upon them, to heap up the gauge-box with aggregate, sometimes moved with misguided zeal to save cement and so their employer's pocket (an attitude not always frowned upon by the employer!) and sometimes due to the simple habit of diddling the inspector. There was plenty of bad concrete, and the evidence can be seen today in the crumbling corners and the weathered faces of old walls. There was also good concrete, which stands today to show what could be done, for such faults as the passage of time has revealed were generally due to scamping, and not to ignorance on the part of the workman.

In spite of modern advances, therefore, it is sad to have to record that since the change to mechanisation and its accompanying methods of supervision, I have seen worse concrete—incredibly worse—than ever I saw in the days of the shovel. Perhaps the most regrettable change that has taken place is that the concrete labourer has come to depend on the machine to do the work— the pushing of a button, the pulling of a lever—and he has lost the craftsmanship of his fathers. On large mechanised jobs, where every stage is controlled by technological supervisors, this fact is not so obvious. It is on the medium-sized and smaller jobs, where more depends on the skill of the labourer, that anyone familiar with the old order can see at a glance that the craftsman's hand on the shovel is sadly missing.

As work on the station platforms advanced the station buildings also began to appear. These were the responsibility of a building contractor, who brought from the city a race of workmen— joiners and plumbers, slaters and painters—who wore overalls and worked neatly, and whose ways and outlook had as much in common with those of the men on public works as the sardine industry has with whaling. There were also building inspectors, decent chaps with whom we collaborated amicably when our respective operations touched, and whose different outlook gave us a new refreshing slant to the more domestic side of construction. There was one hearty man I remember who had a beard, one small son and a lisp. Later, when the line was opened and his inspecting work was finished, he stayed on, and I saw him at different times doing craftsman's work himself—joinery, painting and so on, and he also wore overalls. I knew he had a son because he liked to talk about him.

'My boy!' he said one day, 'I'm going to make him either a plumber or a civil engineer. The plumber,' he continued after a pause for the intriguing alternatives to sink in, 'the plumber is called in by a poor old widow to mend a leaky pipe in her attic that's threatening to ruin her ceiling. He turns off the water, has a look to see what's the matter and then goes home for his tools. He brings back a four-foot length of new pipe, cuts out a chunk of the old one that has been mended several times before, and puts the new one in its place. The new pipe goes into the bill, his time goes into the bill (including going back to fetch his tools), and he walks off with the old pipe and fifteen pounds of valuable solder stuck on to it! Bleth my thoul, Judath wath a plumber!'

He paused to wipe his face, which was warm with the light of battle, and perhaps the memory of Homeric professional combat with some unworthy members of a worthy craft.

'And the civil engineer? You go to the meeting of the County Council or the Town Council or the Works Committee, and they're having a free-for-all about the new scheme. They're all but at each other's throats, and the chairman is banging away with his hammer and shouting for order. Then the civil engineer comes in with a roll of plans under his arm, and he spreads them out on the table and, says he, "This is the way I think it should go, gentlemen", and the whole thing is settled in two minutes and peace prevails. Yes, I think that in spite of material possibilities in other directions, I'll make my boy an engineer.'

He left me, ruminating on the fact that it takes all sorts to build a railway.

20

Mileposts

ORDERS CAME THROUGH one day that we should get on with
the measurement of the line for the erection of mileposts, and it
was arranged that one of the resident engineer's assistants named
Gostwyck and I should do it together. Gostwyck was a slight
little man who wore pince-nez, played the banjo and had a stout
heart. We lost no time in getting under way.

We measured along one rail with a steel band, 66 feet long,
or one chain, marking each length with chalk. The chain is a
convenient unit for measuring mileage, as eighty chains go
to the mile. At each quarter-mile, or twenty chains, we drove
a long wooden peg and marked the distance on it. On the
third day, after a morning spent on other work, we were getting
into our stride again and measuring along between Creagan
Bridge and Appin when Mr. Wilson came breezing down the
line.

'How are you chaps getting along?' he asked. 'How many
miles are you doing in a day?'

'Four or five,' we told him.

'Is that all? When I was doing that job we used to manage
seven or eight in a day.' And off he breezed again.

We might have reminded him that we had other things to
attend to beside measuring for mileposts, but we just looked at
each other and said nothing. Towards six o'clock, as we neared
Appin Station, the workmen's train for Ballachulish slowed
down as it overtook us. The Boss and Mr. Wilson were on the
engine. 'Come along, Kennedy,' Wilson called out. 'Aren't you
fellows going home?'

'No, thanks,' I said. 'We'll just carry on and finish the job
while we're at it.'

It was Wilson's turn to say nothing. He just looked at the Boss, gave us a friendly wave and the train went off.

We had measured about four miles that day, and there were still about fourteen miles ahead of us. It was Friday evening. We released the two labourers who carried the pegs and the hammer, and took two others on from the night shift. Between one and two hours later we were near my lodgings, and broke off with relief to enjoy a hearty supper.

When we set off again the sun was low in the west, and would soon have dipped behind the far hills across the loch. But there would be no real darkness in the short summer night. The light but changed from grey to darker grey as mile followed mile, and lightened again in the small hours, while at every length of steel band our monotonous chant broke the quiet of the night:

'Are you right there?'
'Right here.'
'A-all right!'

Some time in the early hours we stopped for a few minutes and ate a snack, and listened to the soft night sounds that seemed to etch out the silence, the constant whisper of the sea on the nearby beach, and now and again the haunting far-off cry of a sea bird. The few scattered dwellings we passed were asleep, but it was six o'clock and full day when at last we came in sight of my home, and a thin column of blue smoke rising straight up in the still air proclaimed that things in the kitchen were moving. We measured on till we met the workmen's train going Appin-wards, sent back our two labourers, and borrowed two others from the dayshift. Then home for a brief rest and a welcome breakfast.

We could not long delay, however, for there were still about seven miles to go. It was getting on for four o'clock in the after-noon when finally we reached the terminus, logged our last measurement and turned rather wearily homewards. How we travelled the first stretch of the way I do not remember, but I have an idea we may have got a lift for a mile or two, perhaps in the Boss's trap. Being Saturday afternoon there was little chance of our getting a lift on a loco, but when we had covered the first three miles or so we did see one coming from the opposite direction and pulling up near the water tank, where it usually berthed for the night.

'Stop him before he draws his fire! Hey, Ropey!' called someone, and we ran along yelling.

Whether the roperunner did not spot us, or did spot us but was too anxious to get home for his tea, it was hard to say, but I have never known a fire drawn in quicker time, and by the time we reached the loco the crew could only express their regret.

Another four or five miles to tramp. I dropped Gostwyck at the Shelter and had the last mile to myself. That evening I fell sound asleep with my head on the supper table, and when an hour after I had gone to bed my brother followed to the bedroom to see how I was getting along he found me still dressed, kneeling beside my bed and peacefully dead to the world again.

There were about this time two other milestones of different kinds that marked the course of events. The first was chiefly of local interest to ourselves. Mr. Wilson went off to get married, but before he left the Boss gave a send-off party for him at the Ballachulish Hotel. The guests included members of the contractor's and resident engineer's staffs and a few friends from among the local folks. Each, according to his talents, was called upon to contribute to the gaiety of the evening. Those who could sang songs, and some who couldn't did their best. Speeches were made and tales were told. The headmaster of the Ballachulish school played the piano. The Roman Catholic priest had brought his violin, and D. T. Rose his chalks. It was the nearest approach to a Highland ceilidh that could be expected from a party sponsored by a Lowland public works contractor. When in due course Mr. Wilson returned, accompanied by a comely lady, quiet but competent, with a friendly touch to her and crinkly bits of humour in the corners of her eyes, we agreed unanimously that he was a good chooser.

The other event was of wider import than could have been foreseen. The contractor's headquarters were in Edinburgh, and Mr. John Best himself did not often visit the Ballachulish works. On one such visit—it must, I think, have been 1902 or 1903—he brought with him one of those modern marvels that we had all heard about but few had yet seen on the Highland roads—a motor car. At its approach people stood by the roadside and gaped, and horses stood on end and bolted. To the chauffeur who drove it, the car was still something of a wonder, and I recall his attempts to explain to me how his engine worked.

'I reckon,' he said, 'that the first stroke gives her the mixture, and the next one compresses it; then it fires and expands on the third stroke and the fourth pushes out the burnt gas.'

I tried to look as wise as possible, and accepted his explanation without critical comment.

21

Board of Trade Inspection

THE LAST FEW weeks before the line was opened were hectic, and memory of them is rather blurred. Many last-minute jobs had to be put in hand and a constant watch kept to ensure that nothing was overlooked in the rush. In addition to the mileposts the position of gradient indicators had to be set out at every change of grade, and the boards themselves erected. A picture that comes to mind is that of a painter, busy on the expanded-metal fence that surrounded Duror Station, painting hard with two brushes, one in each hand.

Before any opening could take place, however, the Board of Trade had to be satisfied, after an exacting inspection by their representative, that the line was fit to carry the public in reasonable safety on their lawful occasions. This would not mean that the work was finished. Much subsidiary work would remain to be done, as well as general tidying up, and also the making good of any faults that might develop during the period of maintenance for which the contractor was responsible—in our case a year.

On 13th August the official inspection took place. This was the day we had all been working for, a day that we hoped would bring to fruition our labour throughout the years. Especially it was a day of importance to engineers—civil, mechanical and electrical; it was their work that was under test. It was not surprising, therefore, if in some quarters a certain tension could be sensed as we gathered in the morning at Connel. There were representatives of the consulting engineers who had designed the works and supervised their building, of the contractors, large and small, who had carried out the construction, and not least in importance the officials of the railway company, whose child the new line was, who would operate it when once the Board of

Trade had given the green light, and who would finally take it over when the contractors had duly fulfilled their obligations.

Many of those representatives were men of eminence in their own spheres, but none of them held the limelight today. It was Colonel Yorke, Inspector for the Board of Trade, who on this occasion was the principal actor on the stage. Tallish in stature, military in bearing, somewhat aloof, on his decision hung the question of whether the new line was or was not ready to fulfil its function as a public service. There was little doubt in the minds of most of those assembled as to what the issue of the day would be, but some who were most concerned must have harboured a hidden fear lest some mischance might befall, some oversight be unearthed, that could cause delay and mar the success of the day.

First to come under review were the signalling arrangements. On a double-track railway the crossing points wherever possible are laid as 'trailing' points; that is to say the tapered switches are facing away from the direction from which a train is arriving. If trailing points are wrongly set it is unlikely that a train will be derailed. On a single line, however, such as the Ballachulish Railway, trains run in both directions on the same track, so that all points in one direction or the other become facing points. If facing points are badly set there is every chance of a derailment, and special precautions have to be taken to prevent this by locking the points in the correct position. When a signalman wished to go through the procedure for taking on a train he had first to set his points for it, then he threw over the locking bar which locked the points in position. Only then was he able to lower the signal for the train to proceed, as all these movements were interlocked. The locking bar was a light steel section that ran along the inner side of one of the rails and was longer than the wheelbase of any railway carriage. Its function was to prevent the points being moved while a train was running through. Such an attempt might be accidentally due to a human frailty— an absent-minded signalman, worried perhaps about a sick wife at home and suffering from loss of sleep, or one who had gone off his head, or indeed it might be due to evil intent by some criminal who had knocked out the signalman and wished to wreck a train.

Whatever the purpose of the man in the signal box, if he put the signal back to danger while the train was passing through, and then tried to move the locking bar with a view to releasing the points, he could not do so for the wheel flanges of the passing train prevented the movement of the bar.

It was the function of the inspector to look for trouble, to find fault if fault could be found. He gave orders to the signalman to pull levers, to carry out any movements that could lead to the derailment of a train. He was very thorough, and he did in fact find certain features that called for alteration in order to avoid the risk of two trains meeting on the same line within the station limits. Similar tests of the signalling and switching arrangements were repeated at each station throughout the line.

Control of traffic between stations was effected by the operation of the block system. Under this system the line was divided into six sections that ran between the seven stations—Connel Ferry, Benderloch, Creagan, Appin, Duror, Kentallen and Ballachulish. In normal working only one train was allowed on any section at a time. To ensure this a special tablet was issued to an engine crew about to enter a section. This was hung up in the cab of the engine, where it could be seen by both driver and fireman, and it was a serious offence for a locomotive to enter a section without a tablet, except in special circumstances when special instructions were issued to the driver by a higher authority. The tablets were solid metal discs about five inches in diameter. Several of these were kept in locked boxes at each station, usually in the stationmaster's office. Each tablet was perforated in a different pattern, so that, like a key in a lock, it could be inserted only into the box at either end of its particular section. Thus at each intermediate station two boxes were required, and one at a terminus.

Only one tablet could be taken out at a time for each section, and two men were involved in the operation. When a train was due to enter a section, the signalman or authorised member of the station staff gonged ahead to the next station, asking by signal if the line was clear. The signal, like a kind of morse, was made by striking an electric knob on the tablet box and the pattern of the signal indicated the kind of train that was approaching; thus three-pause-one meant a passenger train. The signals for up and down trains had different sounds, such as a bell and a gong, so that the signalman at the receiving end could tell by ear from which direction the signal came if he happened to be out of the office but within earshot. If the line was clear he repeated the signal back, and then the two men operated their knobs together and a tablet was released at the first station. This was put into a leather wallet attached to a stiff loop, taken outside as the slowing train approached, and, as the engine passed, a quick exchange was made with the fireman for the tablet of the section just left. That tablet was at once put back in its box and the section cleared. (This swapping of tablets with a moving train was a routine matter, but had to be expertly done. With the train travelling at some speed it had its hazards and one had heard of a man, perhaps grown over careless with familiarity, having his arm broken by the weight of the swinging tablet. On main line fast non-stopping trains the exchange was made by means of a mechanical arm.) As the train left, a two-bell warning was signalled to the station ahead.

As in the case of the signalling arrangements, the operation of the block system controls was put through a searching scrutiny by the inspector at each station.

The testing of Connel Ferry Bridge was a more imposing affair. Test loading was applied by a train composed of eight Caledonian locomotives and four thirty-ton wagons, giving an aggregate load of about 740 tons. The train was first run slowly over the bridge, with stops at predetermined positions, then several runs were made with increasing speeds. Meanwhile, under the eye of the inspector, a senior member of the resident engineer's staff took a series of levels to record deflections at critical points, first unloaded and then under various conditions of loading. Junior engineers trotted about with their levelling staves from point to point as directed.

The waters of the tidal falls that swirled below the bridge had never seen such an array of man-made power, but they passed on their way unheeding, as if scornfully conscious of the vastly greater power that had swept them to and fro through the narrows from time immemorial. Those of us who were not directly concerned with the steelwork of the bridge were also but onlookers, and took no part in the performance, but unlike the falls we followed with keen interest all the proceedings, and shared in the general satisfaction when the tests were over.

Exception was taken by Col. Yorke to the use of gravel ballast instead of broken stone, and he recommended its removal for a length of 200 yards north of Connel Bridge. In other parts where gravel had been used it should be treated with an admixture of sharp material.

The party now entrained again and proceeded leisurely along the line to Benderloch Station, and after inspection of the safety control installations there, went on to Creagan Bridge. Here similar tests were applied to the bridge as at Connel, but less complicated, as befitted a simpler structure. With the few smaller plate-girder bridges on the line (which were part of Best's general contract) the proceedings were simpler still. Two planed wooden rods, about $1\frac{1}{2}$ in. square, were held vertically, overlapping, underneath the unloaded bridge, the lower rod bearing solidly on the ground and the upper held firmly against the underside of a girder. A pencil line was drawn across both rods. When the girder deflected under the loading of the locomotives a fresh line was drawn, and the deflection measured with a rule.

The day was fair, and as each stage of the inspection was left behind there seemed to be a lightening of any tension that might have marked the morning's beginnings. Col. Yorke had noted that in several places the line was still in an unfinished condition, but it was not suggested that this would affect the opening programme. We had reached a point near Lagnaha, however, when a check occurred, a sharp reminder that the day was not yet over. Here a small, unattended siding had been installed to deal with some heavy local freight, and something was wrong. A small matter, but it involved the locking arrangements that ensured the safety of the line. There was a short conference between the inspector and the railway officials. These were able to give an assurance that the missing part would be expressed to the site at once and the fault made good, and the crisis passed. Near the terminus at Ballachulish we stopped for the test of the last bridge, a small plate-girder structure that spanned the River Laroch. The party got down, the locomotives got into position clear of the bridge and then there was a slight and ludicrous pause; for the stream ran chuckling between the abutments from side to side, and there was no dry land on which a man could stand to record the deflection. It was only for a moment. Mr. Rose grabbed one of the measuring rods. 'Come on, Kennedy!' he called and jumped in ankle deep.

There was no trouble at the terminus. Whatever formalities had still to be gone through, the outcome of the day now was that the Ballachulish Railway would be allowed to open as a public service, but for the present a speed limit of twenty miles an hour would be imposed. When the unfinished work had been finished, ballasting improved and the track consolidated, an increase of speed could then be considered.

The official party relaxed and chatted with one another. The local folk were out to gaze at the animated scene and the imposing array of rolling stock, seen in that setting for the first time, and rejoice in the prospect of more easy contact in future with the outside world. But amid the general satisfaction at the close of the day there was one regret that must have cast a shadow over the hearts of the thoughtful: the Ballachulish strike had not yet ended and around the amphitheatre of the hills the scars of the silent quarries looked sullenly on. The fact that the station buildings were roofed with slates from the quarries of Wales was a sad reflection on the follies of industrial strife.

22

Opening of the Line

ON FRIDAY, 21st August, eight days after the Board of Trade inspection, the line was officially opened. The inspection had been a technical affair, a matter for engineers, and for railway officials concerned with the running of the line. But this was a gala day for a wider public, and important people from many sections of the community were invited to attend. The Caledonian Railway Company, which would operate the running of the trains on the new branch, laid on a special saloon train from Glasgow. It carried a party of some sixty representative gentlemen from Glasgow, Edinburgh and other centres. At Connel the train was joined by another party of guests from Oban, including Provost Cooper. There were present directors and senior officials of the Caledonian Railway Company and its protégé, the Callander and Oban Railway Company, and representatives of other lines as well. But among the hegemony of high-ranking officials whose presence graced the occasion, no name had a higher significance than that of Mr. John Anderson, the Secretary of the C & O Railway. He had fathered that line step by difficult step from its earliest conception through the testing years, and now this addition to his family must have given him a great thrill of satisfaction. Stocky, with a short pointed beard, and now getting somewhat rotund in figure, he carried easily his seventy-odd years, and seemed withal to bear a quiet air about him that spoke of achievement.

The guests included representatives of other transport, such as MacBrayne the shipping people, and of industry such as the Ballachulish Slate Quarries, and in the case of some it was hard to detect their connection in any form with a railway, except as potential travellers.

The firms of engineers and contractors directly concerned with the building of the line were well represented. Sir John Wolfe Barry was there—bearded, large of frame and impressive, and on behalf of Formans and McColl were the partners J. E. Harrison and John Ferguson. For the main contractors John Best was present in person, and Theodore Arrol and Frederick Black represented Arrols Bridge and Roofing Company, who built the steelwork of the two large bridges.

The site staffs of both engineers and contractors, who throughout the changing years had borne the burden and heat of the day, were present in force. We still had our responsibilities, but today they sat lightly upon us. For once we could travel in state along the line we knew so well and view it objectively, as tourists, forgetting the cares of office.

If those who originally pioneered the line had only had in mind the opening up of the country for the benefit of the stranger who wished to come and view the beauty of the Highlands, they could hardly have found in all the land a region more richly endowed.

Westwards of the main loch the mountains of Mull and Morven formed an imposing backdrop, and in the foreground the island of Lismore and the lesser isles of Shuna and Balnagowan interrupted the wide expanse of sea and gave a more intimate character to the view.

The natural features of the landscape—the rugged line of the coast that compelled the railway to its devious course, the encroaching sea at Connel and Loch Creran—these created difficulties for those who planned the line, adding to the cost of the works and providing problems for the engineers. But for the traveller with an eye for rural beauty they had a value of their own. Each curve of the snaking track gave him a fresh aspect of the panorama of mountain, woodland and sea, and as his train passed over each of the two large bridges he was given a glimpse of yet another aspect—the narrow loch stretching away in its channel at either side like a picture seen briefly through the opening of a doorway in a garden wall.

Connel Bridge made a good start for the day's viewing, and at North Connel all got down to admire the imposing structure.

There was much admiration too for the view up Loch Etive, stretching eastwards within sight for some six miles, till away beyond the narrows at Bonawe it turned towards the north and buried itself behind the hills. To its right the mass of Ben Crua-chan, though softened by haze and diminished by distance, stood out like a bastion guarding the narrows, and dominated the horizon.

This is a region that is haunted by legends of the beautiful Irish maiden, Deirdre, who fled to Scotland to escape the attentions of Conacher, the High King of Ulster. She was accompanied by Naoise and his two brothers, the sons of Uisneach. For a time Scotland gave them sanctuary, until in due course they were persuaded by the false promises of Conacher to return to the shores of Ulster. There the three brothers were treacherously slain, and Deirdre came to a tragic end.

Entrained again, we travelled north at a comfortable speed that made it possible to admire the changing views. The day was fine and full of promise, and in tune with the spirits of the party, and also with the hopes of the scattered dwellers in the straths and glens whom the line would serve. Here and there along the route flags were fluttering in the breeze, and little knots of people gathered to see us pass and give a cheer.

At each station the train made a brief halt. Benderloch was the first of these. From there to Creagan was seven miles, the longest section on the line. For the first two miles the sea was shut off by the lowlying land that projected towards the west. Then the line broke out into the open again where Loch Creran blocked its direct passage, and swinging round to the right it wound its way through cuttings and over embankments between the broken coastline and the wooded hill behind till it reached the narrows. Here the bridge carried it over, and once clear of the obstacle that had barred its progress, it doubled back for a short distance to Creagan Station, before cutting across country again to Appin.

The route along Strath Appin was at first less impressive than much of what had just been passed. It ran over moorland, and through the Dirty Cutting that during the construction years had for so long bogged our labours and now looked innocent as a dell. Beyond that the strath spread out into green fields, with scattered houses strung along the course of the public road and a few more imposing dwellings set back in the midst of their broad demesnes. There had been a good deal of rain during the summer, and the harvest was late, but the hay crop was good. Haymaking was well under way and ricks dotted the fields.

At Appin we were back once more within sight of the sea. Immediately in front, in the small inlet of Loch Laich, stood the ruin of Castle Stalker, said to have been for long the home of the Stewarts of Appin. Sturdy and four-square on its half-tide rock, to a stranger viewing it for the first time it might well have looked as if some whimsical artist had planted it there to please his fancy, and form a striking feature against the seascape with its scatter of small islands and the mountains beyond. He might also wonder what dire straits had driven the builder to incarcerate himself in such a place, with scant room for garrison or family and retainers, and no provision for life but possible fish from the sea and the rain from heaven.

The party seemed to be enjoying themselves. Some were no doubt familiar with different places along the route, but few, save those directly connected with the works, had ever travelled it from end to end. They were now enjoying a private view of what three days hence would be open to all and sundry who cared to travel.

The Boss had given me his camera to take a few pictures for him, so I laid aside my own more primitive box and, as occasion arose, took snapshots of groups of the great ones. Regretfully I recall that I never asked him to let me have copies.

Shortly after leaving Appin Station the railway met the public road, and side by side they ran for the next two miles through country uninhabited except by sheep, between the sea's edge and the rough hillside. At the Salachan River the fields began again, and towards Duror Station the picture changed. Cuil Bay at the southern end of the Ardsheal peninsula, lay sheltered from the north, with its few small farms landward, and its three sharp rocky points, Rhu Beag, Rhu Meanach and Rhu Mor—Little

Point, Middling Point and Big Point—lying in echelon, and pointing southwards to the wider seas.

Here once more the track left the lochside, and likewise the road, and ran along the level strath of Duror, past the standing stone at Acharra and through the ripening fields of Acharn that James of the Glen had tilled, till the bulk of Ben Vair barred the way and shouldered both road and railway together again at Kentallen. The little bay lay below, looking peaceful and welcoming. It was pleasant to sit in comfort in the moving train, and remember the early days of footslogging through wind and weather along the hard miles.

At Kentallen Station the new pier, designed to be a direct link between steamer and rail, was not yet finished. Road and rail still clung together and, with brief separation near the Ballachulish Ferry Station, they continued thus until they reached the terminus at Ballachulish.

Here all was gay with bunting, and coaches were standing by in readiness to run the party up to view the famous Pass of Glencoe. There had been delays on the run from Connel. Whenever the train had stopped, and members of the party had got down to admire the view and stroll around, it was no mean feat marshalling such an important and independent flock back to their carriages again, and now the schedule for the day had fallen behind. The Glencoe trip had to be curtailed, and the coaching party, having gone far enough to view the rugged mountain masses that guard the entrance to the glen, turned back at Clachaig Inn.

All now adjourned for a belated lunch at the Ballachulish Hotel. Presiding at the function was Mr. Hugh Brown from Glasgow, a director of both the Caledonian Railway and the Callander and Oban. There were toasts and the making of speeches. When the royal toast had been honoured a certain Councillor MacKenzie from Edinburgh proposed 'Prosperity to the Callander and Oban Railway and the Ballachulish extension', and he extolled the beauties of the line. There were admirable sites all along the way for villas, and he hoped the merchant princes from Glasgow and Edinburgh and other cities would be quick to see the benefits they and their families could derive from residence in the neighbourhood. This optimistic outlook was greeted by a round of applause.

The chairman, in reply, said he remembered very well when the Callander and Oban Railway was originally proposed. It gave rise to a very amusing and admirable paper by Professor Aytoun in *Blackwood's Magazine* entitled 'The Glenmutchken Railway'. At that time it was all very well to make fun of a railway to Oban, but those days were past.

Following the lunch, as reported in the *Oban Times* for 29th August, 'The party afterwards rejoined the train, which was waiting on the line close to the hotel, after an extremely pleasant ceremony.'

The same issue recorded the fact that the line was open to the public on the 24th, and advertised, without comment, the first timetable for the new branch, with five trains running in each direction.

23

A Year of Maintenance

THE OPENING OF the line brought a complete change to our methods of carrying out the work that still remained to be done. We could no longer send an engine up the line at will, but had to comply with the normal regulations for operating—carry a guard's van at the back of the train, with its tail lamp on behind, take out a tablet when the line was clear for our use, watch the clock and avoid interfering with the regular running of the trains. We could no longer use our rough construction wagons, but had to arrange for the use of trucks from the railway company. The company also provided us with loco drivers from their regular staff, and an experienced guard to accompany each construction train. These men knew the rules. They also knew most of the railway staff who had to administer the rules, and they knew how they could be applied so as not to tie us up unnecessarily with red tape—altogether a tower of strength to us.

A lot of the outstanding work did involve our encroaching on the line with construction trains. Embankments had shrunk, and many of them had to be topped up and enlarged to standard width, with filling brought in from outside the area. There had not been time to finish off completely the ballasting of the track before the line was opened, and stone for this had to be loaded up and distributed where required. There was also construction plant collected in depots beside the line which had to be loaded up and removed between trains. There were innumerable minor items to be finished, repaired and tidied up, and finally we had to maintain the line in good running order for twelve months after the opening, and make good any defects that showed up during the period of maintenance.

In the office there was much work to be done on the final

measurements of the many items not yet agreed with the resident engineer. On the questions of fact, such as the quantities of the various items, agreement could usually be reached, but on matters of principle or interpretation of the contract there were many differences that could not be resolved. These would be submitted by the contractor as claims for discussion with the consulting engineers on the completion of the contract, and if not then agreed they might be taken to arbitration.

In the field, too, there was a lot of final measuring to be done, and some of the major items which were straightforward and did not involve much in the way of argument fell to Gostwyck and myself. There was fencing, for instance, which straggled uphill and downdale along both sides of the line from start to finish, mostly wire fencing with iron standards where this was practicable, with innumerable odd bits of post-and-rail at bridges and other breaks where continuity had to be abandoned.

Then there was the railway track. It will be remembered that the rails were provided by the railway company, and this also applied to the crossings, chairs, fishplates, bolts and all the other oddments, except sleepers, that went to form the permanent way. This material had now to be accounted for. We had already measured the line for the purpose of erecting mileposts. We had now to calculate the number of rails, fishplates, chairs and so on that were involved in that length. We had also the sidings to detail, with the points and crossings and all their fitments, and the odd lengths of rail that had been cut to size for special cases. The cut-offs, of all sizes, were assembled and neatly laid out in the goods yard at each station. How long it took to count and measure all these things I do not remember. We had other work to do, but at last the herculean job was finished. It had been laborious but interesting, and called for as much of common sense and tolerance as of mathematics. When we had worked it all out we started checking up to find how much of the track was missing. When we were busy on this Gostwyck's chief, the resident engineer, came to see how things were getting along.

'Have you remembered,' he asked with a mischievous smile, 'to deduct all the expansion gaps between the rails?'

No, we told him, rather shortly, we hadn't done that, and we countered with the remark that if we had we should also have had to remember the occasional special rails on the inner line of curves, which were four inches shorter than standard.

With regard to the expansion gaps, in order to estimate in a precise manner the aggregate length of these gaps we should first have had to find out at what standard temperature the rails had been cut when fabricated, then, as they normally changed in length with every rise or fall of temperature, to find out at what time of year the various sections of track had been laid, and after that to guess whether Bill the platelayer did use the correct gap gauge in every case when he laid the rails at all seasons of the year. Here was a year's food for a gaggle of sea-lawyers, and the end of it all would be the deduction of some three or four rails from the measured length to be credited to the contractor.

The question of arriving at the number of 'specials' laid on curves, though irksome, was a more straightforward affair. We should simply have had to walk the line again, measure all the rails on the inner side of curves and note the number of those that were four inches short. The result would probably show that four or five lengths of rail should be added to the number to be credited to the contractor.

We did not go into these details with the resident engineer; we did not discuss them at all. This was a case where common sense prevailed; we ignored the mathematics and hastily agreed to forget both expansion joints and special rails.

At the end of the day we tallied up. The rails accounted for were twenty-four feet short of what had originally been given us. Twenty-four feet! We checked it quickly over again, but there was no mistake that we could find. We thought of the miles of rail, much of which had been strung along the line for years, of the bits and pieces of cut-offs lying scattered about the station yards for months, and of the mucky corners of bog and embankment where stranger things than bits of rail could so easily disappear.

Looking back now my recollection is that this close agreement applied to the whole of the rails handed over to us by the railway company, both the 32-feet new rails that were finally laid in the main track and the 24-feet second-hand ones that were laid in the sidings. I have no figures to confirm this, and if it were suggested that on this occasion my memory played me false I can only say that even if only the siding rails were concerned the close degree of accord seemed incredible. But that was not the end of it. A few days later I ran into Gostwyck. There was a funny look in his eye.

'Do you remember,' he asked, 'that twelve-foot closer that was put in at Connel Junction?' I did.

'Well, we forgot to measure it!'

A twelve-foot closer meant twenty-four feet of rail. So now we were all square. We had accounted for the exact length of rail that had originally been handed over to us. We didn't believe it. I don't believe it now. There must be a catch somewhere, but it is too late now to go back and hunt for it.

Soon after the opening of the line I changed my quarters to Benderloch, and there for some four months I lodged with the stationmaster. This was very convenient. A good deal of tidying up remained to be done between Benderloch and Creagan. The travelling gangers on both this and the Appin section had left, and I had to take on the supervision that would normally be theirs. We housed our little train in the Benderloch Station sidings, and some of our men lived in the district, so that in every way the station was a good centre for operations. From my bedroom window I could look down on whatever train I wanted to catch, and skedaddle down at the last moment to catch it. On one occasion only do I remember being let down—a Saturday afternoon when I was going home for the weekend. I was finishing washing upstairs, with the train purring away contentedly at the platform, and knowing that I had a comfortable sixty seconds to catch it, when it suddenly gave a toot and went off. The stationmaster had found that his clock was a minute slow and, very unwisely I thought, had put it on a minute while the train was in the station. However, I had a pass to Oban and I took the next train in that direction and spent a pleasant afternoon before making again for home.

For widening of the embankments we got trainloads of ashes from steelworks in the Glasgow area—horrible stuff, full of half-burnt birch brushwood that made it difficult to shovel out of the wagons, but I imagine we got it for nothing; the owners would be glad to get a tip for it. I had a good ganger in charge of this work, a dignified bearded man from Wester Ross named MacAskill, whom I could well visualise when he was at home as a respected elder of the kirk. When there was time enough between trains the ash train would move out on to the section, unload the ashes where required, or as much as there was time for, and clear the section again in time for the next scheduled train. A good deal of time was wasted in this way, but there was no alternative.

I was with the gang on one occasion when we had to unload half the ashes at one place and then move a mile along the line to discharge the rest. When we were about to move I told the men to stay on the wagons instead of getting into the guard's van. At the next stop, when the last of the load was being shovelled out, MacAskill came over and asked a little diffidently why I had told the men to stay where they were.

'To save time,' I said, 'and to give them a chance to cool off.'

'That was a mistake,' said MacAskill, in a voice of mingled respect and fatherly rebuke that could give no offence to anyone, 'a man will never work so well as when he's warm.'

On another occasion when the unloading was half done MacAskill seemed to be getting anxious and suggested it was time we were getting back to clear the line.

'There's time enough surely,' I said, 'we have over ten minutes yet.'

'I think your watch must be slow,' he said.

We compared watches and checked with the guard. Sure enough my watch had suddenly lost ten minutes, for no apparent reason, it had been right when we started. We scrambled on to the train and raced off down the line. This would not do. If we got into the habit of holding up passenger trains we should become very unpopular. Incidentally, my landlord, the stationmaster, was a fusser for regulations, and by this time was probably getting well steamed up. I put up a small prayer, 'Lord, you know it wasn't my fault about these ten minutes . . .'. We reached the station thirteen minutes late. The train was lying at the opposite platform, and Jimmy the driver, with a quizzical grin on his face, was leaning out of his cab, holding up three fingers. He himself with his train had been ten minutes late in arriving.

The old steam navvy had already been dismantled and sent away, but in the broad area of the borrowpit where it had been working some bits of plant that were no longer required had been collected and stored. Alick Woods, the steam boss, was still with me to look after the loading and despatch of these. I was never quite sure what his original training had been—fitter, mechanic, cranedriver? Probably a bit of everything, which was the way on public works in those days.

'If I wanted to get a steam boss for a job like this,' he said one day, 'do you know where I'd look? I'd get a blacksmith. He's a good all-rounder and can turn his hand to anything.'

Little did he guess how soon the race of blacksmiths would almost have ceased to exist, and the smithy become a museum piece and be supplanted by a garage at every corner.

Ballast to make good the slack places on the track we got locally along the line side. This had to be loaded and unloaded by hand, but we also managed to get a limited supply from outside in wonderful drop-bottom wagons that could be unloaded by simply turning a screw and letting the contents run out between the rails at any rate required, while the train moved slowly along the track. When these wagons had been emptied I shamelessly took a turn or two out of them for handling our own supplies before returning the empties to the railway company! Speeding up the operation was all for the good of the job, and no one raised any objections.

We on our part were able in odd ways to help out the running of the trains. There was an occasion when we were waiting at Benderloch Station to get a clear line, when some trouble occurred in the operation of the block controls. An up train was due at Creagan with, incidentally, that redoubtable man Mr. John Anderson, the secretary of the railway company on board, but the tablet box sulked and would not deliver the disc at that end. The reverse operation was tried, and with no difficulty a tablet was got out at Benderloch. The normal procedure in such a case, if no loco was available, was to send a man pelting up the line on foot with the tablet to relieve the beleaguered train. (Why on foot I never fathomed, with a road running alongside and bicycles available, but rules are rules.) That, however, would have caused a lot of delay. We were there, would we take the tablet along?

Our locomotive was an ancient affair with six wheels, the middle pair being without flanges. What its classification would be I do not know. It served our purpose well enough, but it was not the thing one would choose for express journeys. However, we beat it along the seven-mile section in record time and found the passenger train awaiting, with steam blowing off and a much-worried Secretary out on the platform. I expected that we would be taken into the down loop and left there to fend for ourselves till the tablet instrument was repaired, but instead we were directed in to the head of the passenger train. The journey back to Benderloch, with an overdue train and a comparatively powerful locomotive pushing at our rear, not to mention an urgent official anxious to make up time, or at least to ensure that no more time was lost, was certainly no slower than our previous one had been. By the time we reached Benderloch and got uncoupled from our unaccustomed partner the driving pins of our faithful old veteran were glowing a dull red.

Towards the end of the year I was able to leave Benderloch and take up my quarters again at my home; staff at the Ballachul-ish end of the job had been gradually dwindling away, and by early spring they were all gone. I was then left on my own to finish up what remained to be done, and carry on for another half year or so till the end of the maintenance period, with a timekeeper, half a dozen gangers, fifty labourers and a vintage tank locomotive.

Now that the cashier was gone his duties, like so many other things, fell to my lot. Near the end of each fortnight the timekeeper would let me have a note of the amount needed to pay the men, and on the Friday morning I would go into the bank in Oban to draw the cash. On one occasion I asked the teller for ten pounds in silver, and he pushed across to me two tins full of change, which I tipped into the pouches of my money belt. The rest I took in gold sovereigns or one-pound notes.

In the afternoon Donald Livingstone, the timekeeper, and I counted the money and made up the envelopes with the men's pay. The bank had paid me ten pounds too much. The young teller had evidently given me two ten-pound tins of silver instead of two fives as he intended. No wonder my belt had felt heavy with five pounds weight of silver dragging at my waist.

Donald and I went along the line on the Saturday morning and paid the men, and then I took a train into Oban and found my way to the bank. It was closing time, and two of the staff were coming away as I approached. Their faces lit up when they saw me. 'Have you got it?' they cried in unison. I tried to pretend I didn't know what they were talking about, but couldn't keep that up long. 'You'll find him in there,' they said, 'tearing his hair out, trying to get his balance right.' It is seldom that a sight of me has brought more joy and relief to the heart of man than showed in the face of that distraught laddie behind the counter when I opened the bank door.

Half the labour squad were engaged in general work connected with the process of finishing outstanding work and clearing up, the other half were surfacemen on routine maintenance duty. The surfacemen were in gangs of five or six men and a ganger, strung out along the line, roughly in the ratio of one man to the mile. Each gang had its own section, and worked steadily through the section, lining up kinks in the rail, packing up slack lengths or loose sleepers, checking the cant on curves, tightening loose fishplate bolts, keeping the drains clear and free from weeds and generally maintaining the line in good running order. Twice daily a man from each gang walked the length of his section, up one side and down the other. He carried on his shoulder a keying hammer, the head of which had one end shaped suitably for driving in the wooden keys, the other end longer and narrower for driving them out, which was necessary when changing a rail, and on other occasions. Any keys that had fallen out or looked slack he knocked back into the chair. He also carried a few other items such as a spanner, half a dozen fog signals and a red flag. Any irregularity he could not deal with himself he reported to the ganger, and sometimes the ganger himself did the routine inspection.

These men lived as near as they could to their respective sections. Most of them had worked during the construction phase for longer or shorter periods, but it did not follow that every man who was a good navvy shaped equally well on the routine duties of maintenance. These duties called for the steady, dependable type, not the eruptive nomad nor the man who periodically found the temptation of the bottle too much for him. This applied particularly to gangers. Public safety was involved, and if a man who had done good service on construction work now showed that he could not always be trusted to fulfil the responsibilities of his new duties, it was regrettable but necessary to replace him. When in due course the construction work was completely finished and the contract maintenance period had expired, the surfacing gangs would still be required for the upkeep of the line. Those of our men who wished to stay on could then, if considered suitable by the railway company, be taken on to their permanent establishment.

With a good train service, getting around on the line was easy. I usually started the day by walking along the track to the nearest station, up or down, boarding a train and getting off at another station to walk through some section I wanted to see. In this way I could, when I wished, walk over the whole line in about two days, and also get the feel of the track from the engine or guard's van, and any comments from the train staff. They were a helpful lot of fellows and let me know of anything they spotted that seemed to call for attention.

Naturally the young railway had a few growing pains. One very hot day the driver of a down train reported to me at Creagan Station that he had just passed over a bad patch of track about two miles back. It must have just gone wrong, it was all right in the morning when he went through. We set off at once with our old pug engine and the van, picked up the surfacing gang on the way, and dropped them off at the trouble spot. It was at a bend, one of the few stretches where the ballast round the sleepers had not yet been finished. The fishplates had rusted up, preventing the rails from expanding in the rising heat of the day. And so the stresses in the rails had built up until the track had suddenly bulged outwards in a loop of twenty to thirty yards long and over a foot off centre. The trouble was soon put right, and steps taken to prevent a recurrence. Mishaps of this sort did not often happen, but one had to be always on the watch for them, especially in the early stages before the track had properly settled down.

The guard's van was a good place from which to keep an eye on the track in comfort. On each side of the van a panel projected a few inches outwards, thus forming a recess for a seat. In each recess there were two narrow windows, so that by simply turning the head one could look forward along the side of the train or back along the line.

Sometimes, however, I would desert both locomotive and guard's van and travel as an ordinary passenger, mingling with and studying the human tide that flowed into our small creek from the outside world, and listening to their talk. In the summer season the flow became a flood.

There was a man called Houdini, about thirty years of age, an entertainer and illusionist from America. He was at the time widely known as the 'Handcuff King', because of his ability to extricate himself from handcuffs, chains and many other forms of restraint that were put upon him. The guard tipped me that he was on the train, and sitting alone in a first-class carriage, and I went in to have a look at him, but after a glance of mutual appraisal we sat in oppsoite corners and admired the view. An Englishman, military type, watching some hefty Highlanders putting up fencing at Appin Station, murmured to his wife: 'Fine big fellows, if only they were set up with a bit of drill.' A young lady, comely and well-dressed with that quiet simplicity that can be so costly, getting down from a first-class compartment in Benderloch Station, and being met and warmly embraced by an older countrywoman, with a shawl over her head. The variety of interest in those who travelled the line was endless.

A volume known as the Rule Book was issued by the railway company to members of the operating staff. This contained a vast assortment of interesting information, with detailed instructions for such things as station control, signalling, working of trains under all conditions of weather; the use of train brakes—hand, Westinghouse compressed-air brake, called after its American inventor, and the Smith vacuum; maintenance of the track and everything conceivable for the operation of the line and its upkeep in a state of efficiency for the safe transport of passengers and goods alike.

I borrowed a copy from one of the guards, and spent long hours in the evenings delving into its store of treasures. I have seen a modern version of the Rule Book, no doubt adequate for its present purpose, but to me it seems to be but a shadow of the older issue.

There was one unexpected effect that the coming of the railway had on the life of the district. Nothing so swift as the trains had ever been experienced before. Cats, dogs and wild animals had long been adapted to the slower tempo of the horse and were able to take care of themselves, but the train took them unawares, and many were killed on the line. We find the same thing happening again on the motor roads of today. In a restricted area the pedestrian, the law-abiding motorist and perhaps even the domestic pets naturally and subconsciously adapt their movements to the restricted speed. It is then that the irresponsible motorist, blinding along, adds to his armoury the weapon of the unexpected, and thereby adds to his chances of becoming a killer.

It was an ideal life for a youngster. A 'piece' in my pocket served for lunch, and if on occasion I omitted to take it along, a penny bar of chocolate from a slot machine at the nearest station served instead. When walking along the line one found that the 2 ft. 8 in. spacing of the sleepers gave rather a short space for rapid travel, but if one was really in a hurry, to catch a train or keep an appointment, it was best to miss a sleeper, and loping along the line with 5 ft. 8 in. steps it was possible to cover the ground at a wonderful speed. Homing in the evening I would sometimes get on to the engine of the train, the driver would slow down to about fifteen miles an hour at some level spot near my home and I would drop off. I tried, however, to avoid taking too much advantage of the good nature of the train staff. Walking along the line one day I heard a train coming up behind me and stepped off the track. But the train slowed down to a walking pace and the voice of Dugald the driver hailed me in a rich Highland accent: 'Are ye comin' up?' After that I always tried to take cover whenever I heard the distant sound of a train coming along behind me.

There was one driver, Harry, who came to us some time after the line was opened. He was lean and mettlesome as a greyhound, and had been an express driver on the main line till one day he met with an accident. The report was that when moving his locomotive in the station yard he had thrown over his reversing lever, but for some reason the catch had not engaged. When he opened the throttle the lever had sprung back and struck him in the face, knocking out some of his teeth and laying him low. When he came out of hospital he was sent to the Ballachulish line for a rest. It was told of him that on an earlier occasion when he was running a fast train he spied a small bunch of cattle on the fairway right ahead. A crossing gate had likely been carelessly left open. There was no space to pull up, and impact at a slower speed might well have caused derailment. Without hesitation he opened his throttle full and went through the herd like a cannon ball. When he got to the next station his engine looked like a bombed slaughter house.

The first time I met him he wanted to know what speed the line was designed for. It wasn't my business to know that, but I had heard fifty miles an hour spoken of and told him so with reserve. However, when I got home that night I looked up the list of cants prescribed for curves of different radii, and from these calculated the speed on which the cants were based; it was forty. That made no difference to Harry. He went spinning along the section regardless of limits, and the fact that he never had an accident may be taken as a tribute both to his driving ability and to the soundness of the running track. Certainly his testing of the track was in excess of anything imposed by the Board of Trade inspector. The regulations allowed three minutes for station duties, which might include the taking in of water by the locomotive. Harry, however, by saving on the running time, managed to have a lot more time in the stations—up to five minutes extra on a longish section, when he stood by his panting engine chatting with the station staff.

On one occasion, as we ran along between Creagan and Benderloch, Harry told me he had spotted a rabbit hanging on a telegraph pole as he came through earlier in the day, and he wanted to get it.

'I know about that rabbit,' I said. 'I hung it there this morning, found a weasel killing it and put it out of pain.'

When we neared the place Harry slowed down his train to a walk, left the controls with his fireman, scurried across the grass and grabbed his rabbit and was back in the cab in a matter of seconds, tremendously pleased with his prize of a cheap dinner.

Jimmy was also a good driver, but a different type; steady and reliable, although he didn't bother too much about rules for rules' sake. On a rare occasion he let me take a trick at driving his train, which was not in accordance with the Rule Book.

'How do you manage,' I asked him, 'to bring the train to such a quiet stop? One can hardly tell when she's come to rest.'

'Just before she stops I take the brake off, and she glides in to a finish—no jerk.'

The first time I took over the controls we were in the middle of a section, and as we neared the next station I concentrated on the movements of throttle and brake, and managed to pull up without a jerk near enough to where I intended.

'Fine!' said Jimmy. And then an awful thought struck me. 'Jimmy, did you happen to notice when we came in if the signal was down for us?' An impish smile was Jimmy's only answer.

He didn't always manage to pull up his train in gentle fashion. 'Did you hear about Jimmy's adventure on Saturday night?' Beaton, the guard, asked me on a Monday morning.

'No, what happened?'

'He was going round that bend in the rock cutting this side of Creagan Bridge when he saw a man sitting on the rail ahead of him. No, he didn't run over him, he managed to pull up a couple of yards short, but he made all the passengers kiss each other. It was one of your chaps on his way home from the pub, taking a sit-down for a quiet snooze.'

Before Alick Addison left he was on the loco with me on one occasion when it was travelling light. He and Jimmy had been arguing amicably when Jimmy stopped between stations to let him off. 'Thanks, Jimmy,' he said as he scrambled down. Then as he hurried on ahead he threw back a bit of sauce over his shoulder. 'See an' gie that machine o' yours a proper clean up afore I see ye again!'

Jimmy said nothing. Hanging placidly out of his cab in characteristic pose he opened the throttle to proceed on his journey, and as he passed the little man a spurt of water shot out of the injector overflow, missing him with intent by a few inches. Alick gave a yell and a jump that nearly rolled him down the bank, and before he had recovered his equilibrium Jimmy had withdrawn himself like a winkle into its shell, and there was only the unresponsive rear of the receding loco for Addison to shake his fist at.

The up train was in Duror Station one morning, station duties finished, and the guard waved his green flag. But Jimmy at the other end of the train seemed in no hurry to proceed. He was standing on the platform, arms akimbo, chatting to the stationmaster. Knowing his man, Beaton was not worried, but he strolled along to the head of the train to find out the reason for the hold-up. Jimmy, unperturbed, explained:

'When we were down by the distant signal I saw Mrs. Kennedy coming along the road in the machine in an awful hurry. She should be here any minute.' He glanced at the turnip in his waistcoat pocket. 'Och, we can easy make up the time!' He had seen my mother, half a mile from the station, charging along in the trap behind the old hill pony, and decided to wait for her. They wouldn't do that for you in Euston Station even if they *knew* you wanted to catch the train!

Jimmy in due course was moved from the Ballachulish branch and put on the Oban-Glasgow run, promotion, I suppose. The last time I saw him I was on my way to Glasgow, and it happened that Jimmy was the driver of the train.

We had pulled out slowly from one of the stations between Connel and Crianlarich, but we had hardly got beyond the distant signal when the train stopped. At first it seemed to be just one of those traffic stops that occur apparently to annoy the impatient passenger with an appointment at the end of his journey, but presently one or two officials came out from the station, and there was much talk between them and the train crew. After a few judicious enquiries from various quarters, including a very worried-looking Jimmy wending his way to the stationmaster's office, I was able to piece together something of what had occurred. On the previous section the driver had sensed a slight knock in one of his cylinders. He would have liked to have taken his locomotive off duty for examination, but there was no other loco on the spot to take on the train, the nearest was at the next station, about seven miles away. Before this could be got into action and sent along the line a lot of time would have been lost. Jimmy thought that if he carried on quietly he could make the next station, where another loco would be waiting to take over. But he hadn't gone far when the trouble, whatever it was (a loose nut on the piston head was mentioned), got suddenly worse and the cylinder head was cracked. Things were now worse than ever, for before the relief locomotive could be sent down the line the section would have to be cleared. I think they did manage to push the train back to within station limits. Anyhow, the rest of the journey was a good deal behind schedule. No wonder Jimmy looked worried. I never heard what happened to him, and have often wondered. Was he reprimanded and demoted for an error of judgement? I like to think that on the contrary he was promoted and commended for doing his best in a difficult situation.

24

Interlude on Ben Nevis

MY FRIEND NORMAN was through from Glasgow, having escaped from the reek of the city to spend a few days' holiday in the territory of his clan, the Stewart country. We had been talking of hills and glens and tramps among the heather.

'Do you think,' asked Norman, 'you could manage to take a turn up the Ben with me before I go back? I've never been up.'

I pondered this.

'Nor have I. Yes, to your question, I think I might manage if you don't mind it being a night trip. We workers can't take a day off just when we like.'

'All the better. We might see the sun rise from the top. That would be grand.'

'Well,' I said, 'tomorrow is Thursday. What about tomorrow night if it's fine? I have got to be in Oban on Friday morning to get the money for the men's wages. If we get the early boat back from Fort William that would give me plenty of time.'

'Fine,' said Norman, 'let's hope for weather.'

Next morning turned out fair, with some high cloud, but nothing to worry about. With a bit of arranging I managed to get home pretty sharp in the evening, and after a wash and a hasty meal we set off. It was getting on for three miles to the new pier at Kentallen, which was finished and in service, but we shortened the first half by cutting along the railway line and picking up the road beyond the China Quarry at Lagnaha. It was less than a year since the line had been opened, after five years of the bustle and upheaval of construction. It still looked a bit raw and self-conscious, but the scars were healing, and it was beginning to blend modestly with the character of the countryside.

We were nearing the pier when the steamer swung into view

from behind Ardsheal, the throb of her paddles coming clearly over the water in the still air. Her red black-topped funnel struck a bright note of colour against the background haze, and her wake as she approached broke the mirror surface of the loch and tumbled into confusion the calm reflection of the Ardgour hills.

There were a good many passengers on board, for the tourist season was well under way. A small huddle of sheep occupied a forward corner of the upper deck, and near them two young calves lamented plaintively at intervals for absent mothers. Most of the voices that drifted down to us from the first-class deck had the exotic tones of well-to-do folk from south of the border. The day of the motor-bus was not yet, and the universal itch for travel that would accompany it, and would familiarise the Highlander with the accents of Lancashire, Stepney and Chicago, was still a long way off.

Along each side of the lower deck an alleyway flanked the engine pit, and here fragments from first-class and steerage met and mingled, watching fascinated the rythmic pulsing of the big machines. The piston-rods, gleaming with an oily sheen, thrust from the rocking cylinders, in-and-out, in-and-out, looking for all the world like the arms of an imprisoned giant as they gripped and swung the turning crankshaft with mighty fists of steel.

What normal boy is there who will not linger by the way to watch the wheels go round? When he attains to manhood he misses no opportunity of studying the latest marvel of the machine age and watching it at work, in order presumably that he may keep abreast of the times and further his scientific knowledge. Later, when perhaps his figure and civic standing have reached substantial proportions, he is ever ready at the call of duty to array himself in his insignia of office, and in the company of other dignitaries attend the opening of the new power station or the launching of the new ship. But whatever the pretext, in the breast of the seeker after knowledge or underneath the chain that adorns the broad civic waistcoat, it is the fundamental heart of the small boy that beats, surreptitiously eager to see the wheels go round.

At Ballachulish pier most of the tourists got off. They were promptly fallen upon by the usual rival porters, who shepherded their captures to a variety of brakes and wagonettes and carried them off to their respective hotels. Many of them would set off in the morning for the Glencoe trip, returning later in the day to catch another steamer.

We made a brief call at Onich, and less than an hour later we were drawing in to the pier at Fort William, where the steamer would tie up for the night. A motley crowd was on the pier, some to meet friends or collect parcels, others out of idle curiosity.

The massy bulk of Ben Nevis, hooded in cloud, loomed up behind the nearer hill. The prospect of a clear sunrise was not promising; we were prepared for that and would not break our hearts. If it cleared so much the better. From the deck we idly watched while the other passengers went ashore, followed by the livestock. The sheep, released from confinement, made a scurrying dash up the street, like boys escaped from school, till the shepherd's dog at a word from his master streaked ahead and brought them up short, laughing silently to himself in their faces. First we refreshed ourselves in a nearby teashop, and then we strolled off through the town, past shop windows with their tartan wares displayed to attract the passing stranger, past groups gossiping on the street in the warm evening air, and so took the road beyond leading to the Ben.

Among the many types who seek to reach the highest elevation in the British Isles, two stand out in heroic prominence; first those who, for the joy of it, set out at any season, armed with ropes, axes and other climbing paraphernalia, to find and over-come a more difficult route than the last, and then those who once a year lay aside their daily tasks and compete in a race to the summit and back, the best of them covering the fourteen horizontal miles and some five-sixths of a vertical mile in the creditable time of under two hours. We were none of these. For us tonight the easiest route would suffice, and we were not unduly pressed for time. We had walked but a short way when we came upon a bowling green near the roadside, the smooth perfection of its turf giving an effect urban and peaceful amid the rugged surroundings. One game was in full cry and another had just finished and the players were packing up their 'woods' to go home. We stood for a time and watched the play. One old gentleman, who for some indefinable reason looked like a retired lawyer, was an exhibition all on his own and a joy to watch. As he sent each shot towards the jack he followed it halfway along the green, crooning sounds of encouragement, hobbling sideways with short steps and twisting his body in intense sympathy with the progress of the curving ball.

Norman had been a keen player from his early teens. I was not surprised, therefore, when after a brief spell of watching he glanced at the time and gave me a look.

'What about a game?' he asked. 'The sun won't be down for an hour or two yet.'

I was quite agreeable, and we approached the greenkeeper, a stocky fellow in shirt sleeves with a walrus moustache. He was cooperative when he heard our tale, and produced for us the necessary bowls. I was duly trounced, and an attempt to lay the blame for this on the distraction of watching the contortions of the old lawyer was treated with little respect. An hour passed quickly and it was time to go. As we signed the register and said good night to the greenkeeper, he glanced quizzically at the signatures and then cocked an eye towards the Ben.

'Hardy Hieland divils!' he muttered to himself.

The light was fading when we set off again, but this was the last day of June and there would be no real darkness throughout the night. The clouds had crept lower as the evening advanced, and when we struck up the pony track from Glen Nevis the upper half of the mountain was hidden. We paused now and then to glance back at the darkening landscape. A faint smoke still hung over Fort William in the almost motionless air. The muted sounds of a distant locomotive shunting reached us from below, and a curlew called.

Before we reached the halfway lochan the sky had gone and we were shut in by the grey blanket of the mist. It drifted round the mountainside in ghostly masses that broke and formed again in ever-changing shapes, distorting the images of things dimly seen. It clung damply to our clothes, condensing in dew, and more than once it changed to a wetting drizzle. Then we sought the shelter of a friendly rock and waited till the worst had passed. The blanket never lifted, but the light was good enough to let us make our way over the rough stones of the track and avoid stumbling into trouble.

It was getting on towards one o'clock when at last the ground began to level off, and we knew that we were near the top. Irregular banks of snow, one or two feet in depth, showed up out of the greyness, the remnants of last winter's fall. Most of this would disappear in the late summer, before another winter's snow began to lie.

We paused to look around, but in the changing mist everything looked strange and eerie, and there was no sound but the soft sighing of the mountain wind. The scene might have been from some desolate region of the far north. We had been warm while walking; now we suddenly felt the chill of the open summit striking into us and we moved on again. It was then that in the stillness we heard the twittering notes of a bird, at first straight ahead and then fluttering about to one side or the other—an unexpected and friendly sound in the empty gloom. We never saw it, but guessed it to be a snow bunting, that lonely little bird of the high tops. Almost immediately after, we espied a dim glow ahead and this presently evolved as a window of the observatory, the building looming up like a darker greyness out of the mist.

Our knock at the door was answered by the observer, clad in a thick white sweater and looking like an Arctic explorer, and presently we were sitting indoors enjoying the snug warmth of the stove. Thick stone walls and double-glazed windows effectively shut out the chill of the night and also gave a sharp reminder of the bitter weather that could be encountered in that high place exposed to all the winds of heaven.

The observer confirmed our guess as to the identity of our wandering bird. He was a quiet man, not unsociable, but reserved in his talk as one who lives much alone. If I rightly remember, he had a colleague asleep somewhere, whom we did not see. He must have had, for day and night records had to be kept of wind, temperature and weather conditions, but although for part of the twenty-four hours each man would have the companionship of the other, for much of the time he would be alone. Such a life is not for every man, and calls for special qualities of mind.

We were hungry after our climb, and we lost no time in getting out our sandwiches and enjoying a meal in comfort. Presently the man bestirred himself and lit a lantern, and we followed him out into the night and watched while he read his instruments. On a platform giving access to one of these we paused and considered the position. 'Four thousand four hundred and six feet,' said Norman, 'plus about six feet for the platform. You know, tonight we're the highest men in Britain.'

The observer warned us about the escarpment to the northeast, and before returning indoors we crept across crunching snow to where the edge of the plateau stopped short and the mountain fell away sheer for a thousand feet. Beyond was nothing but the swirl of the drifting mist. We threw stones out into the void and timed their fall, listening till the dull crack reached us as they struck the rock far below. We did not linger, for the air was raw and chill, and we were glad to get back to the warm comfort of the fire.

The steamer would leave Fort William at five, and we had seven miles of rocky road to travel. So at three we buttoned up, said goodbye to our host and set off briskly down the track. The greyness was lightening in the early dawn, but the mountain was still hung in cloud. Refreshed by our rest and pleased to get moving again we stepped it out, resigned to the fact that for us there would be no glorious sunrise that day.

And yet the play was not over; for as we descended, the spirit that guards the Ben, perhaps feeling that his reception of two strangers on his domain was not quite in accord with the traditions of Highland hospitality, relented for a brief moment and gave us a parting picture that would long be remembered. We had not gone far on our downward way when we sensed a quickening in the changing of the light. The mist thinned and brightened and then parted suddenly like the drawing of curtains. Far below lay Loch Linnhe, pale and dreaming in the new-washed light of the morning, while all around the cradling mountains were rousing from their slumber and reaching up to catch the first light of the rising sun. And then the cloud curtains swept together again and the scene was gone.

In the end we had to run for it. The gangway had already been run back on to the pier and the ropes were being cast off, but the captain saw us and held his hand, while the gangway was hurriedly pushed out again to let us scramble on board.

All things come to an end. In the autumn I went round bidding goodbye to many friends before setting off for Glasgow and the world beyond. Among the last to call on were the Downies in their cottage across the road from the old smithy at Kentallen. When I left them the old man filled the doorway like a rotund benevolence, one hand deep in the pocket of his white moleskins, the other raised in farewell. His wife, spare and active as a kitten, her white hair covered by a white frilled cap, came out to the roadside to wave me off.

'Goodbye and God bless you,' she called, 'and come back a chentleman, for that's what you are whatever.' Now, could any send-off have been nicer than that?

25

Old Acquaintance

FOR THOSE WHO take part in the building of what used to be known as Public Works (a name regrettably fallen into disuse), be they roads, railways, bridges, harbours, dams or projects of a like nature, it follows that when one such work has been finished the builders must go elsewhere to build another, perhaps in the next county, perhaps at the other end of the earth. Touch is lost with friends and acquaintances, and if, at the end of the day, one wishes to pay a few calls on friends one likes to remember, it may involve at the least a journey around the world.

Among the many with whom I was associated in the building of the Ballachulish Railway, there were comparatively few I ever heard of again, and fewer still I ever met. In Cairo, a year or two after I had left the district, I met, for a few brief minutes, Mr. Schreiber the surveyor. Mr. John Ferguson, the consulting engineer, I met again in Glasgow, and he kindly helped me with introductions to some of his colleagues. Years later, when he had gone to London to join another firm of consultants I met him once again. Rory Matheson, who when we last met him was walking ganger on the Appin section, emigrated—to New Zealand, I believe—and was lost to my ken. Sandy McLean, who had been storekeeper at Kentallen, was, when last I saw him, in a Glasgow hospital again, this time helpless from a stroke, I think. When I asked him if I could get him anything, he wondered if I had an old copy of Molesworth's *Pocket-Book of Engineering Formulae* I could let him have. An easy wish to gratify that would give him many hours of absorbing study.

Mr. Wilson I met two or three times during the winter of 1904–5 in Glasgow. I remember dining with him at the home of his father, a charming gentleman whom I thought bore a strong resemblance to his son, though somewhat balder. I can still see him sitting at the head of the table, and carving the joint with a bland air of dignified competence. Wilson also had me through at Dundee to have a look at a harbour job he was doing there, where he showed me the first beginnings of reinforced concrete that I had seen (or ferro-concrete, as it was then called). Then he too went abroad. A relative in Australia had died and left him Scott's Hotel in Melbourne. He gave up engineering and went out to take over the place. He would make a popular host. Years later I met him in London when he was back on a visit to the homeland: filled out a bit and a trifle balder, but otherwise little changed. Long afterwards, when, as we drove down a street in Melbourne I read on a passing building 'Scott's Hotel', I thought what a wonderful welcome I should have got if he had been still alive.

It was some years after the Second World War had ended and passed to the realm of history that I found myself at Kyle of Lochalsh in Wester Ross, in the company of two people whom I was convoying across to the Isle of Skye. But the day was stormy, and after lunch the couple decided they would be more comfortable if they stayed where they were for the day and viewed the waves from the hotel windows, rather than risk a buffeting on the ferry crossing.

I had no reason to hang around, and turned homewards towards Inverness. But half the day was in front of me, and I remembered that one or two of our old gangers were said to be still living on a croft not far off. I would look them up. The postmaster at Plocton was helpful and very much alive. He knew the men I was looking for and with the aid of a map he directed me on my way. The road was almost deserted, but after a mile or two I saw a lady standing by the roadside and stopped the car to verify where I was. As usual in such cases, whether in city or desert, she was a stranger, newly arrived and had no idea.

Further along the road I overtook a man striding along at a good pace. He wore a sleeved waistcoat and had on top boots. It was starting to rain as I pulled up alongside him.

'Do you know where Kenny Macintosh lives?' I asked.

'Which wan? There's two Kennys.'

I mentioned Ballachulish.

'That's me.'

'Jump in,' I said as I opened the door.

He had a section of the public road to maintain, and was on his way home from work. He remembered me, or said he did, and also other names I mentioned, Addison for example. But of some he was not so sure. 'I'm only seventy-nine,' he said, 'but I don't mind things as well as I used to. Louie has a better memory, although he's eighty-three.'

We would have to leave the car, he said, and walk the last half-mile to the croft. The rain was falling heavily when we left the car, and by the time we had sloshed along the muddy half-mile it was coming down in torrents. Kenny did not seem to notice. A strapping lass met us at the door. She was, I think, the daughter of one brother and niece of the other.

'Where's Louie?' asked Kenny.

'He's up at the hay. I'll go and call him.'

She slipped into her waterproof and pulled on her gumboots. I protested, but she insisted on going along with me to the edge of a field, in the midst of which a man was peacefully scything the grass. 'Louie!' she called. The man stopped and shaded his eyes with his hand. I chased her home and wended my way across the sodden field towards him. He was wearing a jacket, but, like his brother, he seemed to be indifferent to the rain. I introduced myself, and commented on the strange weather in which he chose to do his haymaking. I suppose he had started before the rain began, and just carried on. 'When the weather's like this,' he explained, 'I like to get it cut, and then when it fairs it's all ready for drying. But I've done enough for the day.'

He buried the blade of his scythe in a swath of grass and came back with me to the house, where for a short spell we discussed old times, and then I left them. They had settled back, these two, into the ways of their fathers, as though the interlude of railroad building had never been.

Mr. Rose was the only one of the old gang with whom I was able, with some long intervals, to keep in touch till the very end.

Soon after Ballachulish days he took up an appointment in Malta on harbour construction, and a few months later I saw him there. The cargo ship on which I was travelling to Egypt spent the weekend in Valetta harbour. He showed me round the work he was doing, took me to church, and we chewed over old times.

After the First World War we met again in Yorkshire, where he held an important position on dam building for Bradford Waterworks Department, who were carrying out the work departmentally. We were both married then, and a rosebud had blossomed in the Rose household. We spent a couple of happy days as their guests.

Alick Addison was there on his staff, in his early sixties now, but full of energy still. He had known the district before, when John Best had a contract with Bradford Corporation for an earlier project, and when a few years after our visit he retired, it was in Pately Bridge that he and his wife settled down. After that I saw him only once, when, on a motor trip to Scotland, we turned aside from the main highway to pay them an unexpected call and got a royal welcome. How he spent his years of retirement it would be hard to say, for he was not a reader. But one can draw conclusions from a visit the Roses paid to him, when they found him energetically putting a high polish on the brass tap of the village water supply, which he had evidently undertaken as a regular civic duty.

In 1935 my old chief himself, after fifteen years amidst the Yorkshire moors, retired to Hove in the south of England. Here, apart from the inevitable calls of house and garden, he was able to devote his time to that joyous urge of his life, the making of pictures. Black-and-white, oils, etching: he had tried them all, but water-colour was his favourite medium. He told me once that when some idea caught his fancy and no better materials were at hand, he would try to find some sepia for colour and chew the end of a matchstick to make a brush. When making studies from memory of men at work he would sometimes enlist the help of his wife (and daughter when she was at home) to model for him with pick or shovel, to ensure that he got the correct pose.

For much of my time in the ensuing years duties took me abroad or north to Scotland, but during the long periods when I was back in the London area we met more often than we had done since the early days. On one occasion I remember when Rose was up in town and we were about to walk across the Horse Guards Parade, he paused for a few moments and gazed at the buildings around the square.

'I can never pass here,' he said, 'without stopping to admire the marvellous variety of tones on the walls of these buildings.' The tones were created over the years by the soot and grime of London's atmosphere, lain on to a background of Portland stone, and delicately tempered for the artist's eye by the falling rain. He would, I think, have viewed with mixed feelings the epidemic of cleaning that has since overtaken the public buildings in the London scene.

He lost the sight of one eye, and that proved awkward for a time, but he soon adapted himself to the disability and carried on. He could sell his pictures when he wanted to, but he tried to avoid competing with those whose art was their livelihood. For him it was the joy of creation that mattered. When in the course of time the Roses decided to move to London to live with their daughter, I went down to Hove to help him pack up his pictures, a formidable accumulation. Soon after the move he thought in a whimsical mood that it might be a good idea to make a rough estimate of the number of pictures he had stored in the attic and elsewhere about the place. Stacked together they made a pile three feet high. He counted how many it took to make an inch in thickness, and then calculated there were about 3,000 in all. Half of them were painted on both sides of the paper.

D. T. Rose was blessed with a keen but restrained sense of humour, and also a sympathetic awareness of the merits and failings of the men who laboured under him, and the hardness of the life that many of them had to lead. Both these qualities of humour and understanding are apparent in many of the sketches he made of the navvy and his like.

The outlook of the artist and that of the engineer are often antagonistic: the one sees visions and other sees facts. In Rose's case, however, the qualities of both were complementary: the artistic sense did but enhance his ability as an engineer. He died in 1964, two years before the death of the railway he had helped to build.

26

Inquest

WHEN THE END came at last to the Ballachulish Railway I was on a visit to Scotland, and I had a nostalgic urge to have one more trip along the line: it was over half a century since I had last travelled it. But it was a day of heavy rainfall, I was a hundred miles away at the time, and I let it go. The last train ran and a bus service took over.

There was a sudden outcry among the local people when it was found that the bus had not the same facilities for handling parcels as had been provided by the train, and someone had forgotten to arrange for the transport of milk from the farms.

These were matters that could be remedied, but there was something almost indecent in the haste shown in pulling up the track, as if to make sure beyond all doubt that the line could never be used again. Two months after its closure I read a press report that half the track was up, and it was expected that in two months more the work would be finished.

I was still minded to revisit the scene of so many early memories to learn what I could of the reasons that had led up to the summary closing of such a public service and to see what effect the change had made in the lives of the scattered folk the line had served. A year and a half slipped by, however, before the opportunity arose: just as well, perhaps, for by that time the upset of change was over, and the new pattern of transport along the route had settled down.

At Carstairs I left the train from Euston, was met by a nephew and driven to Lanark, and in the morning his wife and I set off in her car for the north, leaving the good man to fend for himself for a day or two. At lunch time we ate our sandwiches in October sunshine by the side of the 'new' Glencoe road. The tourist season was nearing its end, and not many cars passed by. Ahead of us the scarred form of Buachaille Etive stood out against a sky of chastened blue and soft fleecy clouds. A slight rise in the ground to our right concealed the spreading waste of the Moor of Rannoch, while away above on our left, running round the flank of Meall a Bhuiridh and the Black Mount, could be discerned a thin line that could be none other than the old road over which I had bicycled so many years before.

We checked in at the Glencoe Hotel, and went out to make the most of what was left of the day. The number of old acquaintances who were still alive was sadly depleted. I should find it was like that all along the line. But others, though strangers, were friendly and willing to talk about their transport problems. One old man in the Glencoe village, housebound and sitting by his fire, had been a nipper with one of the gangs in the early days of construction, and later a member of the Ballachulish Company of Volunteers. Frail of body but clear of mind and intelligent, he was full of interesting reminiscences.

The Ballachulish terminus, once a scene of such bustling activity, was empty and desolate, like so much that we should see as we went along—buildings falling into disrepair, odd scraps of discarded material lying around to trip the unwary, because it was not worth the salvaging, and no one seemed to have thought of amenity.

At Kentallen a part of the station building was still in use as a tearoom. We were the only clients, and the girl in attendance had plenty of time to chat, and give us her views on the railway question. At Duror Station we turned back, to spend the night at our hotel.

The morning met us with a downpour of rain and a flat tyre. From Ballachulish Hotel, three miles away, a man came to mend the tyre, and without too much delay we were able to push on down the line again. Intermittent heavy showers continued, with rain, hailstones and claps of thunder, but as the day wore on the weather bettered, with longer clear spells. From time to time we stopped to examine some special feature of what had once been a railway, or pay a call in the passing at one of the scattered dwellings.

M

Near the centre of the Duror Strath, where the river swings in to touch the edge of the public road and bends away again, stand two small houses joined together. Over the past hundred years they have functioned as dwellings, and at various times have housed such public services as school in the first place and later as shop and post office. A little to the northwards the river is crossed by a steel bridge that leads to Acharn. Opposite the bridge we pulled up under the trees to consider for a bit and let a heavy shower go by.

I remembered someone down south who would be thinking of us and wondering if any fresh fern roots would materialise from this trip. She knew the journey was for business purposes and not for pleasure, and had thoughtfully refrained from mentioning the subject of ferns. But I recalled what years had passed since she had last had an opportunity, in the passing, of raiding, with the owner's consent, the ferny crannies of Dalvaniach Rock. The rock today was too far off, but I knew of a small outcrop just across the river where the wrens used to nest and a few ferns grew. The rain still fell, but I scurried across. As I was about to climb the fence by the muddy roadside a car drew up behind me and a friendly lady who was driving it asked if she could help me. I learned that she and her husband owned the place. I told her what I was after, and she invited me to take anything I wanted. They had not been long in possession of the farm and now regretfully were leaving because of the difficulty of getting staff. The Forestry Commission were taking over.

'You know,' I said, 'that your fields grow the best potatoes in the district.'

'So they tell us,' she said, 'but what can we do if we can't get the men to work the land.'

Near Appin Station the row of half a dozen substantial houses that had formed the heart of the hamlet of Portnacroish stood blind and empty, three of them being now used only for summer visitors. Nearby, in her neat cottage I found an old friend I had known as a small girl when the line was building. She was now a widow and lived alone. Public-spirited and active in such affairs as the 'Women's Rural', she was now not quite so active as she had been. As we chatted on matters past and present, her grandson, a bright youngster in his teens, looked in to see her and do her messages. Since the closing of the line it was not so easy to get goods sent in from outside. Her late husband, as a lad, had worked as a chainman with the survey party that set out the line, till their operations reached too far from his home. One of his jobs was the numbering of the index pegs, and I remember that his neat figuring had been shown us by Schreiber as an example of how it should be done.

At Creagan Station I lingered. I had watched it take shape from start to finish. In the arched subway that gave access to the island platform the concrete, protected from the weather, looked smooth and perfect as though it had been placed there a month before. But outside, where it had been exposed for a lifetime to the onslaught of sun and wind, rain and frost, any corners that were not perfectly sound were beginning to show signs of weathering, and in places the weeds were trying to get a hold. Around the entrance the scrub was crowding in, as one sees the jungle do more swiftly in a tropic land, when human life has been withdrawn from human habitations. The station buildings stood empty and neglected, and on the platforms the grass was growing.

We drove round the head of Loch Creran, a five-mile detour compared with footing it across the railway bridge. At the head of the loch a new road bridge was being constructed. There had been appeals from the public to carry the road across the now disused railway bridge and so avoid the detour, but the government view was that the cost of the diversion, including heavy work on the approaches, would be greater than could be undertaken with the funds at present available. In the meantime the new bridge at the head of the loch was necessary.

Short of the railway bridge we paused by the roadside where we could view it while we ate our lunch—stately as ever it seemed, and at one with the landscape, but silent now from the sound of the passing train, and shorn of its purpose.

'I'm going up to have a look at it,' I said. Mat throughout the trip had been the perfect driving companion.

'Anything you wish,' she answered. 'I'll go on ahead and wait for you beyond the bridge. Leave me with a bit of water to look at and I'm happy for as long as you please.' I left her with all Loch Creran to dream over.

As I clambered over the railway fence and up the high bank of the approach, now overgrown with a jungle of shrubs and small trees, I passed a dead sheep at the foot of the slope. It seemed a fitting part of the picture—the stricken beast lying down to die by the side of a dead railway.

I crossed over to the north end of the bridge, my footsteps on the deck scarcely sounding in the empty stillness. The rock cutting beyond swung out of sight to the left in a yawning curve. It was here that Jimmy, driving the late night train in that first year of the line, had thrown his passengers into each other's arms, and so had narrowly avoided destroying a homeward-bound reveller, who was sitting on the rail enjoying a quiet nap.

I here remembered a scare I had got over the setting out of the stonework at the end of the bridge. The steelwork of the north span ended at the masonry pier that supported its landward bearing, but beyond that the high stone parapets with pilasters at their ends ran on over the arch of the approach. The parapets had been nearly completed when I remembered that the line began to curve almost as soon as it left the steelwork, thus narrowing the gap between it and the inside parapet. The criterion here was that there should be ample clearance to ensure that there should no be risk of the parapet being struck by an open carriage door, making due allowance for the swinging of a carriage or the temporary irregularity of the track. I must have reported the matter to Mr. Wilson, and after consideration it was decided that there was still an ample margin of safety and the parapet might stand as it was. A little thing, perhaps, but one of those things that kept the section engineer constantly on his toes. An examination now showed that we were right: there was no sign of a scratch on the parapet. Here as elsewhere on the bridge the stonework could have done with some repointing of the joints, but apart from that it was ready to serve for another generation or two without attention.

At Benderloch a heavy and prolonged thunderstorm prevented me from taking other than a cursory glance at the station. There was little loss in this: what could be seen was but an untidy repetition of the stations we had already passed. Moreover, the storm compelled me to prolong profitably my visit to a well-informed member of the local community I had called to see.

Connel Ferry had deteriorated from a busy junction to a wayside halt. Back along the trail of the vanished railway my enquiries had elicited the belief that, some time before its closure, British Railways had issued a statement to their stations giving details of the previous year's operation of the branch. I might still perhaps be able to find a copy at the Connel Office. At Connel I found two men working in the yard among a mass of tumbled debris, evidently the sole survivors of the station staff. They were helpful and obliging, as were all whom one troubled for information, but none had heard of such a statement. One of the men hunted with me among the papers scattered around the office, and finally directed me to the telephone—the only thing in the building that seemed to be alive—so that I could make contact with someone higher up The contact proved to be very fruitful, although the existence of the statement I sought was disclaimed.

Workmen were busy at Connel Bridge, converting the deck for the purpose of road traffic only—a single lane for cars and a footpath, at best a makeshift. I walked back over the bridge for a leisurely inspection, and spoke to those in charge of the alterations. Their work was nearly done.

That night at the Falls of Lora Hotel I asked the lady who appeared to be the hostess if she had any connection with the Mrs. Stewart who owned the place when last I stayed there. 'When was that?' she asked. I told her. She paused for a moment with her head on one side, thinking back.

'That was my grandmother,' she said.

We were leaving the next day, due at Lanark in the evening, but the morning was free, and there was one more contact I wanted to make before we left. We had been at school together, but a long time had elapsed since last we met, a chance encounter in a Glasgow street. It was, I think, soon after the end of the First

World War, when the Air Force had allowed him to return again to civilian dress. Now he lived a score or so miles from Connel. I rang him up. He answered at once, as if he had just been waiting for the call, and we made a date for coffee with him in the morning.

The heavy rain had channelled out parts of his approach road, but we found that he had been up betimes filling in the worst places with boulders so that with care we could safely pass. He welcomed us warmly at his castellated eyrie perched on the top of a small hill: changed a bit, and I was surprised to find that his locks were greying, but still he was full of vigour, although he had now given up most of his public interests. The years fell away as we discoursed on things past and present, including what had been the Ballachulish Railway, while his wife and Mat made common cause on other matters of interest.

On the way back we stopped to have lunch in Oban, which had not greatly changed in appearance with the passing of the years. 'The McCaig Tower' still crowned the amphitheatre of the bay like the Colosseum in Rome, but the railway station seemed to have lost its dominating influence in the life of the town.

I had travelled north from London with a purpose, but no one in the district traversed by the Ballachulish Railway knew I was coming. I had made no appointments, just jotted down the names of a few I would like to see, and left the rest to chance. In the circumstances it was strange how fortune favoured me, it was almost uncanny. I met all whom I had wanted to meet, and some of whom I had never heard before, but to whom I was directed as likely to be helpful in any enquiries. When I called on one such stranger at his business premises, he was pointed out to me at once, and when I introduced myself he gave me unstintingly of his time. When I knocked at a cottage door it was opened by the one I was seeking. When I telephoned an official of British Railways, it was he who lifted the receiver at the other end of the line. Even the farmer, setting out with his dogs to go the round of his stock—if I had been five minutes later I should probably have missed him, but I did not miss him. The railway signalman should have been asleep in bed, for he was on night duty, but it happened to be the last day of his holiday, and he was at home alone and very much awake. He was a travelled and knowledge-able man, and he knew well the line that now was closed. He dropped the household repair job he was doing to give me an interesting half-hour of his time.

In reviewing the opinions given by such a varied section of the community as to the effect of the closing of the line, one would have expected a wide divergence of view. But what was in fact most striking was the extent to which the various views were in accord. There was general agreement that the change from train to bus made no very great difference to the local travelling public. Most people now had cars of their own, and latterly few passengers had been using the railway, except for about sixty pupils who travelled daily to school in Oban and returned in the evening. These were said to prefer the railway, for they could move around in the compartments of their train, and some were able to do their homework on their way home. It was remarked by one observer that there was more horse-play than study, but at least those who wished to study had the opportunity to do so. Moreover, since the buses took over they had to leave home earlier in the morning. People again who had no cars had more difficulty now in getting their parcels sent in. There was a complaint that the roads had already been unfit to cope adequately with the heavy summer traffic, and the closing of the line had made things worse.

It is only fair to say that some, living a long way from a station, were said to find the new service an improvement, as they could be picked up or let down at their own doorstep. These presum-ably lived by the roadside. If they lived a little way off they would have to remain without shelter by the roadside while awaiting the arrival of the bus. What proportion of the public were benefited in this way I do not know, as I met none. But for those encountered, from the humble cottager with no car to the responsible official, who might accept the change as a regret-table necessity brought about by force of circumstances, for all these the disappearance of what has been affectionately called the 'Gaelic Express' was a matter of regret. Whatever strong feelings had earlier been aroused, they spoke of it now with quiet resignation, as of the passing of an old friend.

Looking back on these contacts I am reminded of that old poem that many of us learned at school, 'The Enchanted Shirt' by John Gay. Here is described the search of the king's messengers throughout the land for a happy man, in order to borrow his shirt, to cure the king's malaise.

> Wide o'er the realm the couriers rode,
> and fast their horses ran,
> And many they saw and to many they spoke,
> But they found no happy man.

In regard to the closing of the railway I found on my journey no happy man, no happy woman. If they are to be found I did not meet them. Perhaps the general feeling was best put into words by a thoughtful businessman in Ballachulish:

'When the train came in there was always a bit of a stir. The papers came in, you met people. The line was a link with the outside world and kept us alive. Now the contact is broken and the place is dead.'

Sentiment can be a powerful force in the lives of men, but we must guard against being so unduly carried away by it as to be blinded to the hard facts of existence that may force us to changes we would fain avoid. Let us, therefore, briefly examine, as impartially as we can, the facts that led up to the closing of the Ballachulish Railway.

The arrival of the internal-combustion engine has had a profound effect in these islands, as elsewhere throughout the world, on the means available for the transport of passengers and goods. Over long distances air transport has perhaps made the most spectacular advances, but in the vast network of inter-communication it is the road vehicle in all its various forms that has influenced most deeply the lives of the people.

When, away back about the year 1902, I first saw a motor car, I little dreamt that in my time this curious road machine would have gone a long way towards eliminating the horse from the land and ruining the railways of the country, so that so many of the most attractive of them, built with high hope and creative vision, would be threatened with closing down. And who could have foreseen that this same machine would also have destroyed so many of the Highland steamship services? Where, for example, at the turn of the century, busy steamers, carrying passengers, goods and livestock, ran through sunshine and storm between Oban and Fort William, calling at all the intermediate piers along the route, these piers would in less than fifty years be marked by a few rotting stumps, and the place where the gay coaches awaited the laughing crowds of tourists would be deserted and grassgrown. It is little comfort to remember that a century before the impact of the motor car the railways themselves had brought ruin to the canals of Britain, or that the steamship had driven from the seas the gallant race of sailing ships.

The rapid rise in the popularity of the motor vehicle since the first decade of the century has been matched by a corresponding decline in the traffic carried by the British railways, both in passengers and goods. Goods traffic by road has the advantage that much of it can be carried from door to door without tranship-ment from road to rail and rail to road again. On the passenger side the man who owns a car can often use it for business or pleasure with more flexibility of movement than if he travelled by train, and the man who has no car may find the coach or bus more to his liking than the railway, when he goes about his daily business or tours around the country on holiday.

Traffic on the Ballachulish branch declined to such an extent that towards the end of 1963 the British Railway Board published a notice of their intention to discontinue the local passenger train services between Oban, Connel Ferry and Ballachulish on 2nd March, 1964, subject to any objections that might be raised, the consideration of which by the Transport Users' Consultative Committee and the Minister of Transport might cause delay. Objections were in fact raised, and were considered by these authorities, and the proceedings delayed the closing down of passenger services till 26th March, 1966.

As for freight services, it would appear that the British Railway authorities have power to withdraw these facilities without any prior consultation, so long as they provide some other means of transport. The bulk of the freight latterly carried on the branch was material connected with the aluminium works at Kinloch-leven—incoming raw materials and outgoing products. Between Kinlochleven and the railway terminus at Ballachulish transport was by road. In 1965 the Kinlochleven traffic was rerouted over the West Highland Railway via Fort William, and this move, together with the closing of the passenger services, is claimed to have effected a substantial overall economy.

I do not know what measures were considered for continuing to run the passenger services in a more economical way to meet the declining traffic. Small diesel trains have in similar circum-stances been run for many years in other parts of the country as well as abroad. In discussing the matter with an official of British Railways I recalled that as early as 1935 I had travelled across France from Nantes to Dieppe in a small two-compartment train, operated by one man who drove perched up in a small cupola in the centre of his train. Beneath his cabin was a small lavatory for the use of the passengers. I remember that we travelled along at a steady speed of two kilometres a minute or about seventy-five miles an hour, a speed incidentally much in excess of the maximum permissible on the Ballachulish line. Surely a shuttle service with a small train of this sort would have been worth considering, with some or all of the intermediate stations unmanned as a matter of economy.

If in fact such a change had been introduced, and in due course still showed an adverse balance in terms of money, let us remem-ber that factors other than receipts and expenditure must be considered in order to get a true estimate of the value such public services have in the general life of the community. By withdraw-ing a popular service and thereby taking the heart out of a scattered rural people, a heavy item has been incurred on the debit side.

Those responsible for the policy of the Post Office take a more statesmanlike view of their function. The cost of carrying a letter from London to the Shetland Islands must be greater than delivering one to the man in the next street, but the charge to the public for delivery is the same, and no one would suggest it should be otherwise.

One of the crucial questions that is ever with us is the depopulation of the rural districts, the constant movement of people from the country to the densely populated centres, and anything in reason that can be done to arrest or reverse this tendency will be for the good of the country at large. It is sometimes thoughtlessly asked why the townsman should be taxed for the benefit of those who prefer to live in the wide spaces, far from the town's amenities. It is not for their benefit but for that of the country as a whole, and especially for the dwellers in towns. To the countryman the town with its cultural centres, its shops and its factories is a great convenience, but to the town the countryman is a necessity. Basically he is necessary to produce food for those who live in close-packed communities and do not produce their own. A less necessary but important function is to provide food and shelter for the townsman when on his holiday he goes afield to seek relaxation in the peace and quiet of the countryside. And the countryman himself, living among such conditions as allow him time to think, even in the midst of his daily work, may have something of his own to contribute to the culture of the town: Thomas Telford, the first President of the Institution of Civil Engineers, was the son of a border shepherd, and Robert Burns the poet was a ploughman.

One may well question whether even in normal times any state can long survive that has not its roots firmly embedded in a healthy rural community. For an island nation the need is greater, especially in times of crisis, which today seem to be always lurking round the corner. If, for example, our cities, towns and factories were obliterated by enemy action, the rural population could still exist, as did their fathers. But if on the other hand our island were ringed in by hostile forces and our foreign supplies cut off, as so nearly happened in the last war, and if there was no adequate home production of food, the country would capitulate or starve.

Country life is not for every man. The majority would seem to prefer being herded together in urban centres. And, therefore, when a man is prepared to live by choice in the quiet of the open spaces it is well to encourage him. If he is to serve his country in this way it must be possible for him to live and to bring up his family under conditions that he finds tolerable. Otherwise he will fend for himself. If he is denied at home the opportunity to exist he will reluctantly fold up his tent like the bedouin and go to seek opportunity elsewhere, as so many of his kinsmen were compelled to do in former days.

In the Highlands of Scotland, with a comparatively thin scatter of population, and where it is harder to extract a living from the reluctant earth, the depopulation has been most marked.

If this trend is to be arrested, one of the first needs is the maintenance of adequate facilities for outlying districts at reasonable cost—transport for passengers and goods, as well as such things as electricity and telephones. On the transport side there is something of security and dependence in a railway that a road does not give, especially in severe wintry weather. Perhaps the fixity of the track and the strict discipline imposed on railway working have something to do with this, as well as any difference in the comfort of travel. The parents of those pupils who travelled daily to their school in Oban might well feel disquiet at the loss of their railway. As for the pupils themselves, the children of today are the parents of tomorrow, and it would be tragic if such a promising packet of human seedlings should be discouraged by worsening services from taking root in the soil of their native district. And so, when contemplating, because of falling revenue, the closing of a branch railway that has built itself into the countryside and into the lives of the people we should proceed with caution.

Are we then to retain indefinitely all outdated means of communications for reasons that may in the main be sentimental? By no means. Let each case be treated on its merits with due consideration given to human values in the balancing up of credits and debits.

When the Ballachulish branch was closed the track or permanent way was torn up with precipitate haste, thereby casting to the winds such potential capital value as remained of the cost of building the line—cuttings blasted out of the hard rock, embankments consolidated to stability by the passage of time, innumerable bridges, the track itself with its ballast, sleepers and rails, and the stations, with their buildings now rotting into unsightly dereliction. All these works cost in their building what in terms of our present debased currency would run into millions of pounds, and now, unused, are but an eyesore.

It is true that if in the near future local changes should occur, such as the development of new industries, that would justify the reopening of the line (an unlikely event), it would be possible to relay the track and restore such operating installations as were necessary, but at a cost many times greater than the scrap value recovered from the disposal of the old materials.

If, therefore, in the future it is thought necessary to close any of those other railways that have formed a lifeline to outlying communities, let us remember that the public are the owners, and first let a statement be issued giving facts and reasons for the closure in language that the public can understand. Secondly, if a line is closed, let the track be maintained in position for a period of years, say five, so that the effect of the change on the lives and economy of the people affected can be observed and a further report issued. It will be remembered that before the line was originally built an act of parliament giving permission for its building had to be passed. It is reasonable to ask that due care is taken before the line is finally taken away. Such a period between closure and removal of the track should at least extend beyond the next general election, and thus minimise the risk that national assets of importance to local communities might be dispersed by a government that does not possess the confidence of the country.

The Life of The Railway

by George Simpson

THE FAMOUS AREA of North Argyll, immortalised by R L Steven-son's *Kidnapped*, with its romantic scenery was prime tourist country but virtually inaccessible to all but the most determined of travellers. Thus, it was hardly surprising that the Callander and Oban Railway Company had set their eyes on the territory north of Loch Etive, encompassing the districts of Benderloch and Appin, long before their railway reached Oban in 1880. However, another twenty three years was to pass before the opening of the Ballachulish Branch Line on 24 August 1903.

With the opening of the line, travel in the area north of Loch Etive was completely revolutionised. It became readily accessible to tourists who were able to enjoy spectacular views from the comfort of a railway compartment. A Summer Excursion from Oban to Glencoe, via Achnacloich, Loch Etive and Glen Etive, involving train, boat and coach, through some of the finest and most impres-sive scenery in Scotland, became a popular circular day-tour, oper-ating daily, except Sundays, by incorporating the Ballachulish Branch into the itinerary.

As well as tourists, the residents of Appin and Benderloch greatly benefitted from the railway – shopping in Oban, a facility previ-ously enjoyed by the privileged few, quickly became popular, commuting to work, and children travelling to school, also became customary. Another benefit was the transportation of mail by rail, improving the service and its reliability. In addition, a GPO letter box, carried in the Guard's Van of the mid-morning train from Ballachulish, allowed locals to post mail at stations en route, thus giving letters intended for the South of England, a good head-start, to ensure next day delivery.

When Connel Ferry Bridge was built, a footpath was provided alongside the railway track but members of the public were not permitted to use it, and instead had to cross the bridge by a service train. Despite mounting pressure from all quarters this situation lasted until 1909, when a twenty-three seater motor charabanc was adapted for passenger service on rails, to increase the service across the bridge. The charabanc was also capable of handling up to two, four-wheeled flat wagons to accommodate cars and the service was extended to Benderloch, as there was no siding at North Connel. The charabanc made ten, regular, return trips every day, with four of them extended to Benderloch on weekdays, and five on Sundays.

These charabanc services continued until 1914 when approach roads were constructed and the bridge modified to carry a single track road, alongside the railway line. As there was insufficient clearance between them, the passage of road traffic was restricted to the intervals between trains and this practice continued until closure of the line. However, a toll was imposed on all vehicular and pedestrian traffic crossing the bridge, in order to recover the cost of the modification work.

Two additional stations, of wooden construction, namely North Connel and Barcaldine Halt (and Siding) were opened in 1904 and 1912 respectively, and trains called at them, in the main, on a request basis. While North Connel appeared in the main timetable, and could readily accommodate full length passenger trains, Barcaldine Halt only appeared as a footnote and could barely accommodate a single carriage.

From the outset, the colour of the steelwork on all the viaducts was a mustard yellow. This gave the large bridges at Connel Ferry and Creagan a very distinctive appearance. The steelwork continued to be painted this colour until after the grouping of the Railway Companies in 1923 when the London Midland and Scottish Railway Company (LMS) took ownership of the line. However, between then and the outbreak of World War II, in September 1939, the colour was changed to grey, which gave the large bridges a degree of camouflage and, undoubtedly, afforded them protection from enemy aircraft, attracted to the area by the large naval shipping presence in Loch Linnhe.

Construction work on a spur line, west of Connel Ferry Bridge, to allow trains, from Oban, to run directly to Ballachulish and vice-versa was never completed. Hence, the practice of reversing the direction of all through trains at Connel Ferry Station was continued until closure of the line. The reversal process which involved running locomotives around their coaches explained why locomotives hauling passenger trains out of Oban chimney first (forward direction), ended up running bunker/tender first from Connel Ferry to Ballachulish, and vice-versa.

Pattern of Passenger Services

On opening, a daily, except Sunday, service of five passenger trains in each direction operated between Oban and Ballachulish, but this was a summer season timetable, and during the rest of the year there was a basic daily service of only three trains each way. With the onset of World War I in 1914, the summer timetable was abandoned and the basic daily service ran all year round until 1927. From this date, a summer excursion train ran until World War II when the timetable was once again reduced to a basic daily service of three trains in each direction. It was not until after nationalisation on 1 January 1948, that the train service began to resemble that which had been introduced initially with five trains each way on a summer Saturday.

During the fifties and early sixties a basic weekday service of three passenger trains in each direction was supplemented with a late service on Saturdays. During the Summer, a daily excursion train provided an extra service in each direction. The Summer 1962 daily, except Sunday, service is shown on the next page.

		am	am	pm	pm	pm
Ballachulish	dep:	7.14	10.45L★	12.30E	4.25AM★	6.57SO
Oban	arr:	8.48	12.28pm	2.06	6.19	8.30

		am	am	pm	pm	pm
Oban	dep:	8.25M	9.42BE	12.05	4.55	9.20SO
Ballachulish	arr:	10.07★	11.14	1.38★	6.31★	11.02★

Key:-

A/B	–	Forms part of Glencoe, Glen Etive, and Loch Etive circular tour (A – Outward via Achnacloich; B – Outward via Ballachulish);
E	–	Excursion train (Summer Only);
L	–	Conveyed GPO Letter Box;
M	–	Conveyed Mails to/from Appin;
SO	–	Saturdays Only;
★	–	Connection to or from the South provided at Connel Ferry.

On Saturdays, an evening excursion fare to Oban was available on the late afternoon train from Ballachulish and, around 1960, this cost 2/8 from Creagan. This fare was aimed primarily at cinemagoers and allowed them to return home on the last train from Oban which was usually a "happy" one with most of its passengers returning from an outing to the "big smoke". At Connel Ferry this train had to wait on an Oban bound train, from the south, to form a connection to Ballachulish. As often as not, the Oban train was delayed due to late running connections or bad coal or a combination of both. When a prolonged wait at Connel Ferry was anticipated, some passengers would seek the hospitality of the nearby Falls of Lora Hotel. Eventually, after the arrival and departure of the train from the south, a signal of repeated toots on the locomotive's whistle was used to warn the strays of the train's imminent departure. If this failed to return them, as happened on occasions, it fell upon the guard who was responsible for the train and its passengers, to round them up and shepherd them back on board. As the train stopped at the stations en route to Ballachulish, the passengers who were unable to alight by their own efforts were helped off and either laid out on station seats, or on barrows, for their families to wheel them back home.

Freight Facilities – Services & Specials

The "goods" left Oban as a light engine about 3.30am (latterly around 4.15am) to collect its load of wagons from Connel Ferry. Unlike the passenger trains, goods locomotives left Connel Ferry in the forward direction (chimney first) to give the footplate crew shelter from the elements, on the exposed sections of line, particularly north of Appin. Goods trains were well laden, with at least twenty wagons daily, destined for Ballachulish and the British Aluminium Company at Kinlochleven, besides other freight. After leaving Connel Ferry it ran non-stop to Benderloch and after shunting, proceeded non-stop to Creagan. Northbound, goods trains never stopped at Barcaldine because the siding layout precluded shunting. Wagons for Barcaldine were shunted off at Creagan, picked up by the afternoon southbound goods, and then shunted into Barcaldine siding. Upon departure from Creagan the goods proceeded to Ballachulish where it arrived about 7am, after shunting at stations as necessary.

After shunting duties, the goods left Ballachulish around 1pm on weekdays, (7.30am on Saturdays), called at stations to shunt as necessary and arrived at Connel Ferry at around 3.15pm (9.20am on Saturdays). However, with the surge in the demand for aluminium during the late 1950s and early 1960s, the goods locomotive, on a Saturday only, would often make a second trip to Ballachulish, running as a special, in charge of a load of alumina wagons. It returned to Connel Ferry, again as a special, leaving Ballachulish around 1pm and, after depositing its wagons there around 3pm, returned to Oban.

The only other goods specials were from Creagan Station during the Spring and Autumn livestock sales in Oban, if there were sufficient cattle wagons to form a train load. A light goods engine from Oban would collect them, leaving Creagan Station around 7.15am, and proceed to Oban, via Connel Ferry, picking up cattle wagons at Benderloch if required. If, however, there were insufficient cattle wagons to form a special train at Creagan, they were shunted onto the early passenger train from Ballachulish. The schoolchildren loved it when this happened because they knew their train would arrive late in Oban and, in turn, they would be late for school. They were absolutely delighted in the early 1960s when the locomotive from their train became derailed, at the points in the loop siding of Creagan Station, while picking up cattle wagons. It was almost two hours before their train eventually left Creagan Station, after the locomotive had been jacked back onto the track and rejoined with its coaches.

Motive Power

Passenger trains were mainly hauled by Caledonian, Class 2P, 0–4–4 tank engines, affectionately known by train crews as "Pugs", but by the late 1950s these tank engines, first introduced at the end of the nineteenth century, were at the end of their working life. Hence, in summer, with additional services, pressure to find reliable motive power sometimes resulted in goods locomotives being pushed into passenger service. To relieve this situation, three Class 2MT, 2–6–0 locomotives, known as "Moguls", came into Oban in summer 1961 to work on the line. These engines provided an interim solution to motive power but, despite their presence, tanks still continued to haul some passenger trains until dieselisation in summer 1962. While passenger train tanks always took water at Creagan, apart from the 1.38pm arrival at Ballachulish which topped up at Connel Ferry, the "Moguls", with a large water capacity in their tenders, did not require to do so.

Goods trains were hauled by the Caledonian "Small Goods Class", Class 2F, 0–6–0 locomotives until the late 1950s when the surge in the demand for aluminium increased the loading on the freight trains. To meet this demand they were upgraded to Class 3F, 0–6–0s which handled all freight services until dieselisation.

Steam on the Ballachulish Branch was virtually wiped out in mid-June 1962 when the BRC&W, Sulzer, Type 2, diesel locomotives arrived to take over both passenger and freight service workings. However, the excursion train continued to be occasionally hauled by a "Mogul" steam locomotive over the summer months, until September 1962, when dieselisation was completed.

The steam locomotives which hauled the Branch trains for

almost sixty years were sadly missed by all, even those who were not served by the line. Communities on the western side of Loch Linnhe and the northern shore of Loch Leven could mark the passage of time by the smoke and steam from the trains on the opposite shore. With the loss of steam the line lost a lot of its character but the diesels had to come, and the economies associated with them allowed trains to run for almost another four years.

The Fifties and Sixties

Camping Coaches were re-introduced to the Ballachulish Branch line after an absence during World War II. They were stationed at Appin and Kentallen in 1953, Benderloch in 1956 and Creagan in 1958. Although only single coaches were provided initially, they were soon doubled up to meet the huge demand for this popular type of holiday accommodation.

The line was cut twice in the 1950s, the first time for about three months when the line was breached by flash flooding at Barcaldine, in early Summer 1953, and the second time, for under half that period, when the line on the shore of Loch Linnhe, north of Appin, was washed away by a ferocious winter storm, in early 1957.

All stations and Creagan Bridge received their last coat of paint in Spring 1957. The painters were a jolly Glasgow based team who stated that they would not be back. They were right – they never came back.

Dr Beeching's recommendation that Branch lines should contribute more towards their running costs resulted in substantial fare increases in the early 1960s. This, together with the elimination of reduced fares and evening excursions, effectively reduced passenger traffic (at Creagan, a uniform day return fare of 6/6 to Oban, was introduced) and thereafter it just dwindled away.

Summer excursion trains ceased after the Summer 1962 season and, although the Camping Coaches at Creagan were withdrawn in Autumn 1962, those at Appin, Benderloch and Kentallen were in situ until Autumn 1965.

After dieselisation, there was an apparent boost to traffic on the

Ballachulish Branch, when West Highland trains were diverted onto it, on occasions, when their line, north of Crianlarich, was blocked with snow. On arrival at Ballachulish, passengers and freight were then motored to Fort William. Prior to this, the weight of the steam locomotives used on the West Highland line precluded diversions onto the Ballachulish Branch.

Freight facilities were gradually withdrawn between May 1964 and June 1965 but it was the re-routing of all goods associated with the aluminium industry in Kinlochleven, from Ballachulish to Fort William, which finally sealed the fate of the line.

Thus, in mid-June 1965, with no freight and few passengers, apart from schoolchildren, the line was ripe for closure but passenger services continued for almost another ten months. The line was eventually closed after the last passenger train, a special, left Ballachulish around 11.30pm on Saturday, 26 March 1966 and, with the line gone forever, another chapter of railway history was ended.

Acknowledgements

I WISH to record my grateful thanks to all who in various ways, not otherwise acknowledged in the book, helped me with information or enabled me to verify some doubtful facts: To Mr. G. R. Barbour of the Scottish Records Office in Edinburgh for the co-operation of himself and his staff in getting access to the early records of the Ballachulish Railway, both before and during its construction. To Mrs. Forrester and Mr. Stewart of the staff of Messrs. Valentine of Dundee, who gave me every assistance in searching through the large stock of photographs under their care. To Mr. A. E. Cameron, editor of the *Oban Times*, who gave me the benefit of his wide experience. To the officials of British Railways Scottish Region, who were most co-operative in giving me the facts relating to the decision to close the line; especially I am grateful to Mr. Robert Wilson, Area Manager, Oban (since retired), who read the last chapter and gave me his helpful and critical comments. To those among the local folk who gave generously of their time to answer queries regarding the loss of their railway, and especially to Mrs. Mary MacColl and Mr. Jack MacLaren. To Mr. Graham E. Langmuir for permission to use the photograph of MacBrayne's paddle steamer. To Miss Peggie Lockett who helped me with the correction of the proofs. And finally to Miss Margaret Rose, who very kindly vetted the script while it was still in the making, and gave me the benefit of her sage criticism, and has also allowed me to use as illustrations the pictures made by her late father.

DK, 1971